# Acupressure Cure For Common Diseases

Acupressure, literally the method of applying pressure to certain areas or nerves, is one of the safest, simplest and remarkably effective methods for relief from pain and other common ailments. Although using the same pressure points and relying on the same channels of energy, unlike acupuncture, which involves piercing of the skin with needles, acupressure treatment merely requires application of pressure, sometimes both pressure and massage, to stimulate the 'sites' or nerves. The efficiency and effectiveness of this technique has been tested and proven, both in the East, where it has been widely used and practised over the centuries, and in the West, where its advantages have now been acknowledged. When properly applied acupressure not only relieves pain and tension, but can successfully treat complaints as varied as arthritis, headaches and migraines, haemorrhoids, menstrual cramps, impotence, frigidity, back problems, constipation, hypertension and anxiety, asthma, sore throat and sinus trouble. Since no needles are involved it is easy to learn and use, and can be safely practised at home.

The author Keith E. Kenyon, M.D. is the product of University of Southern California School of Medicine. Ever since more information about acupuncture techniques and results became available in the West, Dr. Kenyon's interest in the results being obtained by acupressure grew. When convinced that the benefits were genuine, he undertook formal study of acupuncture at the Acupuncture Research Institute, College of Acupuncture in Los-Angeles. He practises acupressure therapy and general medicine in the USA.

Rs. 35.00

# Acupressure Cure
## for
# Common Diseases

Dr. Keith Kenyon, M.D.

*To Boadi from Duni.*

ORIENT PAPERBACKS
A Division of Vision Books Pvt. Ltd.
New Delhi • Bombay

ISBN-81-222-0008-7

*Acupressure Cure For Common Diseases*
*(Originally published as Pressure Points : Do It*
*Yourself Acupuncture without Needles.)*

© Keith E. Kenyon, M.D., and Paul Winchell 1974

Photographs Copyright : Vision Books Pvt. Ltd.

Cover Design by Vision Studio

Published in arrangement with
Arco Publishing, Inc.
215 Park Avenue South, New York, NY 10003

Published by
**Orient Paperbacks**
(A Division of Vision Books Pvt. Ltd.)
Madarsa Road, Kashmere Gate, Delhi-110 006

Printed in India at
Ravindra Printing Press, Delhi-110 006.

# CONTENTS

FOREWORD      7

1   The Technique of Pressure
    Acupuncture      11
2   Pains from participation in Sports,
    Arthritis and Related Diseases      16
3   Elbow Ailments      19
4   Back Ailments      25
5   Wrist Ailments      35
6   Knee Ailments      46
7   Ankle-Foot Ailments      54
8   Neck and Shoulder Ailments      60
9   Obesity      69
10   Impotence      75
11   Headaches including Migraine      82
12   Sinus Trouble and Sneezing      88
13   Toothaches      92
14   Menstrual Difficulties      97
15   Insomnia and Anxiety      100
16   Sore Throat and Wind Pipe
    Irritation      105

| 17 | Abdominal Pain | 107 |
| 18 | Asthma and Cough including Hiccoughs | 113 |
| 19 | Chest Pain | 122 |
| 20 | Bed Wetting | 125 |
| 21 | Fainting (Syncope) | 127 |
| 22 | Dizziness, Ringing in Ears and Deafness | 130 |
| 23 | Excessive Sweating or Polyhydrosis | 133 |
| 24 | Urinary Problems, Constipation, Diarrhea, Strokes and Hypertension | 135 |
| | PRESSURE POINTS CHART | 137 |

# Foreword

Although newly found interest in the People's Republic of China has focused attention on the subject of acupuncture, it had not been an unknown procedure in the Western World before that. It has also long been known, both in China and outside, that it is not always necessary (and sometimes not even desirable) to pierce the skin with needles to obtain a beneficial result from stimulating the acupuncture sites or loci.

Indeed, physiotherapy machines manufactured in this country many years ago had offered anatomical guides as to where the body should be massaged to gain the greatest relief for the various disabilities which physiotherapy treats. These points were called motor points, and they correspond amazingly close to many of the points on the Chinese acupuncture charts. Furthermore, at least some of the benefit that certain western-type therapy such as chiropractic and osteopathic treatments achieve can be attributed to stimulating the acupuncture sites.

It must be understood that although the word acupuncture comes from the Latin and means to pierce the skin with a needle, and almost all of the publicity about the art centres around needling (which is the closest translation of the Chinese meaning), there are other ways to stimulate the acupuncture sites. At this stage of our knowledge of this ancient and still mysterious treatment, the needle with or without electric stimulation still is the most sensational form of therapy and is the most widely used. However, stimulating the sites with ultrasonic waves, placing direct heat (moxibustion) into them or over them, sewing catgut from one site to another, using suction cups over the sites, injecting the sites with chemicals to irritate and stimulate them, all have been tried with success, although with various degrees of morbidity.One of the simplest, safest, yet still effective methods of stimulating the sites is called pressure acupuncture or acupressure — an Oriental massage in which the fingers are pressed on particular points of the body to ease aches, pains, tension, fatigue, and symptoms of disease, and it is with this form of treatment that this manual is concerned.

The advantages of such a method of treatment are self evident. The possibilities of home use, optimum repetition of therapy and greater safety become clear. The only question that may remain to the prospective user is will it be beneficial? The answer to that is a qualified yes. Qualified because needle acupuncture itself will not work on everything, not even on everything that some of its advocates claim it will. Nor will pressure acupuncture work on every disease. But it can be of great benefit for those diseases which its nature has designed it to treat. And it can treat certain things better than needle acupuncture can—if it is correctly used.

If at this point the reader becomes alarmed that the points will be difficult to find and the proper treatment difficult to administer, his mind should be placed completely at rest. The points are very easy to locate and the treatment easy to apply. However, the very fact that the treatment is so easy to perform and, for certain things, so effective leads to a danger. The danger I refer to is that the reader may tend to self-diagnosis and use this book in place of securing a proper professional diagnosis. There are times that such a delay in securing the services of a licensed physician could result in prolonging an illness or even preventing life-saving treatment from being instituted in time. Although such occurrences are rare, the instructions in this book should only be used on properly diagnosed conditions or in an emergency while one is waiting for a physician to arrive.

When correctly utilized, pressure acupuncture can perform vital relief of pain and rehabilitation of limbs, including tennis elbow. It can relieve many types of arthritis, back pain and sciatica and many other every day ailments. It can prolong one's ability to perform athletics such as golf, tennis, swimming, skiing and bowling. It can be used in conjunction with other treatments for a whole variety of general illnesses such as menstrual cramps, abdominal disorders, help in recovering from strokes, an aid to reducing swelling or edema, and even benefit some neurological disorders. More serious illnesses will require one's own physician and other supportive measures, especially potentially threatening illnesses including asthma, bronchitis, chest pain and several of the diseases mentioned above. This will be clearly described in the chapters relating to those illnesses.

But even without seeing a physician frequently, a person can continuously rehabilitate his joints and muscles, while he is punishing them by vigorous exercising required in sports, by using pressure acupuncture during and after the athletic engagement. This assumes that the person's cardiovascular status would allow such exercise.

Nearly twenty years of medical practice have taught me one thing above all else. Good health can be had if a person works at it, and the simplest treatment is often the best.

Keith Kenyon

# 1

# The Technique of Pressure Acupuncture

**T**he term pressure acupuncture is virtually self explanatory. It means placing pressure over the acupuncture site. Sometimes both pressure and massage are adviseable. However, pressure can be used without massage but not vice versa.

The first question is what is the acupuncture site? The answer is it is a small nerve that is most often embedded in or near a muscle or tendon sheath which serves to attach a muscle to a bone. Therefore, it can be anywhere from one quarter inch to two or three inches below the skin. It somehow is hooked up to other acupuncture sites, and there is considerable argument today about just where these sites fit into the general theories of the human nervous system. This subject we will leave to professional medical journals. Suffice it to say that these sites are real and that by stimulating them we can often help the body in the healing process.

Now it is obvious that sites that appear from one quarter inch to several inches below the surface will require different pressure techniques. It is also obvious that the sites closest to the surface can respond to pressure and massage easier than the deep ones. Fortunately most of the points we will be dealing with are relatively close to the surface.

A second thing to note is that the acupuncture site is a circle about one centimetre or three eights of an inch in diameter. Therefore, one must press and massage an area quite specific in location. Locations will be shown in detail. Frequently there will be a measured distance from an easy-to-find, prominent anatomical part. Since each person has his own body symmetry, a unit of measurement such as an inch can cause gross inaccuracies in locating a point three eights of an inch in diameter. The Chinese found a solution for this by picking a part of the human body that was closely proportional to the individual's general anatomy. They called this measurement a "tsun"—the distance between two points on the middle point of the middle finger when the middle finger is completely bent. Fig. 1 Since this measurement is · somewhat awkward to utilize, an approximately comparative unit is the breadth of the individual's finger. Three tsun are considered to be approximately four fingerbreadths, two tsun, three fingerbreadths. See Fig. 2.

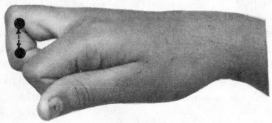

*Fig. 1*
The "Tsun"

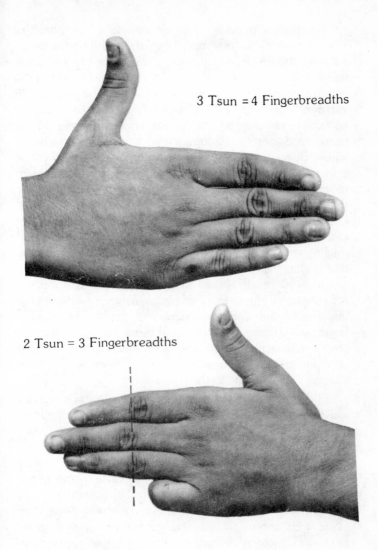

3 Tsun = 4 Fingerbreadths

2 Tsun = 3 Fingerbreadths

*Fig. 2*
*Approximate equivalents of fingerbreadths and Tsun showing where to measure fingerbreadths.*

Thirdly, the pressing of the acupuncture site should be directly over it, and any massaging of the site should be by rotating the finger in a narrow circle over the site while maintaining firm pressure. As a general rule the acupuncture site is more tender than the immediate surrounding area. The feeling of relief that one gets by rubbing a just injured part of the body is largely due to pressure against the acupuncture sites in the region of injury. By placing pressure and rotational massage over the principle specific sites after the first general rubbing even more relief can be obtained. The pressure may vary because the strength a person can persist in using is not constant. One must keep in mind that some of the acupuncture sites can be quite sensitive since they overlie nerves. When a tingling feeling of electricity passes down the course of the nerve which has an acupuncture site which gets stimulated, a beneficial result should occur, since this is a desired achievement. However, if firm stimulation results in very unpleasant pain, less pressure should be used. Besides the finger, which may tire easily and be awkward to apply in places, a knuckle can be a very satisfactory substitute. In addition to these there are electro-mechanical acupressure massage instruments in the market.

Finally, the method of naming the acupuncture sites must be considered. A layman would be completely confused by the Chinese method of nomenclature, since points on the arms and legs are named for internal organs. The Chinese have discovered that there exist over one thousand points on fourteen meridians or lines going up and down the body. We are going to be concerned with somewhat over sixty of the most important points. To avoid your confusion, they will be named by their gross anatomical location. Where there is more than one point on an anatomical area they will be assigned numbers (for example elbow point 1, 2, 3, etc.) Each point will be

14

illustrated clearly. Frequently the same point will be used in more than one illness, and an illustration of that point will then be repeated to make it as convenient as possible for the reader to use the manual. For those whose technical minds need satisfying, the list of illustrations (page 123) provides the Chinese meridian nomenclature compared to the gross anatomical nomenclature.

# 2

# Pains from participation in Sports, Arthritis and Related Diseases

Arthritis has many forms and people suffer from it to various degrees. Amongst some of the Apache Indians in Arizona it is an especially tragic illness since it can affect children of eight and nine years of age with its most crippling aspects. For the most part, however, arthritis becomes worse as one ages, and the youth are not particularly involved with it unless they abuse themselves as some athletes do, especially major league baseball pitchers, contact sports players and tennis players. Pressure acupuncture can help the sufferer of arthritis whether traumatic, rheumatoid or osteo, and it can help bursitis and tendonitis as well as any ligamentous injury that is not severe enough to require surgery. However, the individual with severe impairment should not rely on pressure acupuncture or even needle acupuncture alone but should use it as adjunct therapy to more orthodox treatment as prescribed by his doctor. If the patient expresses the wish to his doctor that he wants to try the treatment outlined in this manual for additional relief from his affliction and shows the manual to him, the physician no doubt will cooperate with him, advising him to be duly cautious as he tries it. The specific therapy that is to be used for these type conditions will be described in the next pages under a discussion of how to take care of such disabilities while actually engaged in athletic events. It must be kept in mind that a severely crippled arthritic differs from one who is still able to play golf only by degree, and that the treatment for both as far as pressure acupuncture is concerned is the same. We will, therefore, proceed to the discussion.

For the young person, athletics are or should be very important. But since young people tend to play intensively they are prone to injury in any running, swinging or contact sport they may undertake. They also tend to enjoy sports they can play most of their lives, but when they are young they may play them more vigorously. Again, injuries can be the result, and an effective method of restoring the injured part to health is of great value. Pressure acupuncture can be of considerable assistance in achieving that end. For the person who is approaching or has reached middle age, proper exercise is important to health and well being. Not only is exercise necessary to keeping us muscularly fit, it enables the body to consume ingested fats quickly and efficiently (as well as starches) so that hardening of the arteries is delayed. It becomes difficult to do this when one suffers from arthritis, bursitis, tendonitis or a pulled muscle in a limb that is essential to carry out the exercise. There are a variety of names for such maladies, such as tennis elbow, pulled hamstring, charley horse or sacro-iliac trouble. They all mean one thing. The individual can no longer painlessly serve a tennis ball, swing a golf club, throw a bowling ball, ski, cast a fishing line, ride a bicycle, jog across country and so forth. Some of the most popular of these sports will be discussed individually, and in that way the various ailments that can afflict the sportsman or arthritic will be illustrated. Younger people may not suffer as much from arthritic ailments as their elders, but they are certainly susceptible to

17

sprains and muscle pulls for which pressure acupuncture and acupressure massage can be a very useful treatment. And it can be used not only out on the playing fields but in the comfort of one's living room while watching television.

# 3

## Elbow Ailments

**L**et us talk about tennis first. Although in tennis the back, arms, legs and ankles can all be injured, the elbow is the most likely target for trouble. Tennis elbow can develop in anyone playing the game because of the severe strain put on the elbow in serving and placing the ball. It must be kept in mind that the tennis racket is an extension of the forearm, and the combination acts as a lever arm for which the elbow is the fulcrum. The longer the lever arm, the more strain on the fulcrum. If a ball travelling rapidly toward the player is struck with the racket, the entire force is transmitted to the elbow. That is bad enough, but frequently even worse injuries are suffered when the ball is missed by the rapidly travelling racket.

Whenever the player feels a strain on his elbow while playing, he should massage and place pressure on the acupuncture sites of the elbow each time the ball becomes dead. If he does this he may prevent tennis elbow from occurring either if it has not already occurred or is a chronic problem with him. The procedure is mandatory while he is playing if he wants to minimize trouble.

## Tennis Elbow

The hand on the non-affected side must grasp the affected elbow and the index finger placed over elbow point 1 (fig. 3) and the thumb over elbow point 4 (fig. 4). The elbow may be either held straight out or bent. As much pressure as can reasonably be applied for 10-15 seconds plus rotary massage is used. One point at a time may be stimulated, if desired.

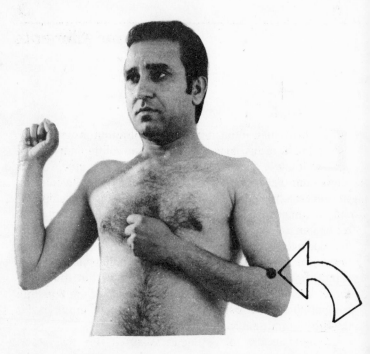

*Fig. 3*
***Elbow Point 1*** *(Large Intestine 11): Located at the depression of the end of the fold which appears when the elbow is bent 90⁰ and raised to a horizontal position. The end of the crease is where the point is located.*

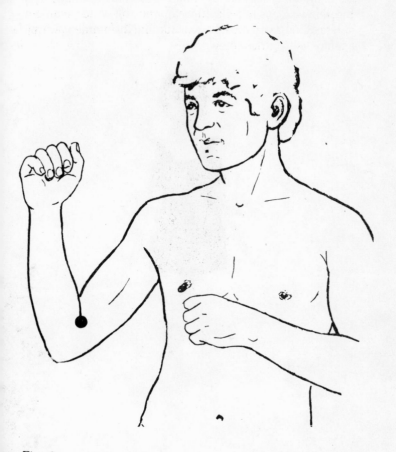

Fig. 4
**Elbow Point 4** (Heart 3) : Located on the indentation near the inside elbow fold next to the tendon on the inside of the upper arm; the end of the crease is where the elbow point is located.

Rotary massaging also can be used to see if it gives added relief. When longer periods are available, longer times, five or ten minutes sessions for example, should be employed. If the elbow begins to feel better, tapering off of the treatment can be done, but it must be re-instituted the moment a strain again is felt on the elbow.

Fig. 5
**Elbow Point 2** (Lung 5) : Located in the elbow fold, on the radial side of the biceps. The point is on the elbow crease at the outside (lateral) portion of the tendon. See also fig. 87.

The other important and useful points elbow 2 and 3 (figs. 5 and 6) are on each side of the insertion of the biceps tendon. The points may be pressed simultaneously or individually, whichever works best for the patient.

Another point, elbow point 5 (fig. 7), is useful, to be used either individually or in conjunction with the previously described sites. It must be emphasized and re-emphasized that in order to get relief from these troublesome ailments, effort must be applied. Repeated applications of pressure with or without massage (whichever affords the most relief)

*Fig. 6*
***Elbow Point 3*** *(Pericardium 3): Located by bending the elbow part way and locating the biceps tendon, which is the thick band you feel in the middle of the front of the elbow. The point lies under the elbow crease at the inside (medial) portion of the tendon.*

must be done. When you are sitting watching television or while at the movies or riding a bus or any activity that does not require both hands, you should apply the treatment intermittantly, reasonably often.

The reward will be great in cases with restoration of the affected part either to complete health or at least with an excellent chance to have a much more bearable infirmity. Once maximum relief has been obtained, occassional pressure will keep the part in optimum repair and possibly reduce its susceptibility to re-injury.

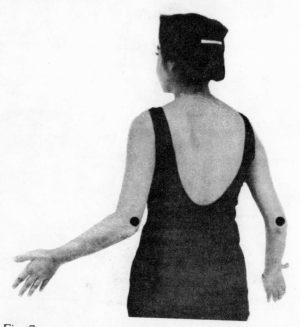

*Fig. 7*
**Elbow Point 5** *(Tripple Burner 10): Located by bending the elbow and feeling for the depression two fingerbreadths above the point of the elbow on the back side. Point is located in the centre of the depression.*

24

# 4

## Back Ailments

The shoulder, which is important in many sports, is closely involved with the neck and will be discussed prior to neck problems. Although golf can involve other injuries, the back is a prominent target. The golf swing is a complicated movement involving multiple muscles and parts. The low back is most likely to be affected. This can be a cumbersome area to treat by the involved individual unless he is particularly double jointed. Nevertheless, most of the points can be reached, and those too difficult to be reached by oneself would be reachable by a willing friend or spouse. Back points are pressed on both sides at once (bilaterally). The most important point, back point one, is illustrated in fig. 8.

Trigger points are points that are tender but are not acupuncture sites. A set of trigger points for low back pain are located as described in figure 9. Identified as back point 2, these points are the most difficult for a person to press or massage himself, and help is needed. As a matter of fact most back points can best be stimulated by second party and especially for a weak or infirmed individual, any point should be stimulated carefully by an informed and conscientious friend.

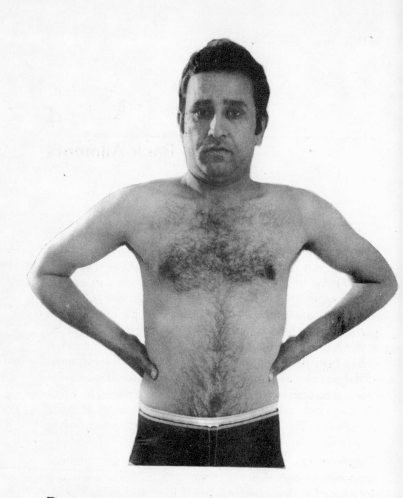

Fig. 8
**Back Point 1** (Bladder 23): *Exact location is between second and third lumbar vertebrae, just behind navel. To make it easy, these points are located on each side of the spinal column, each point lying about two fingerbreadths to*

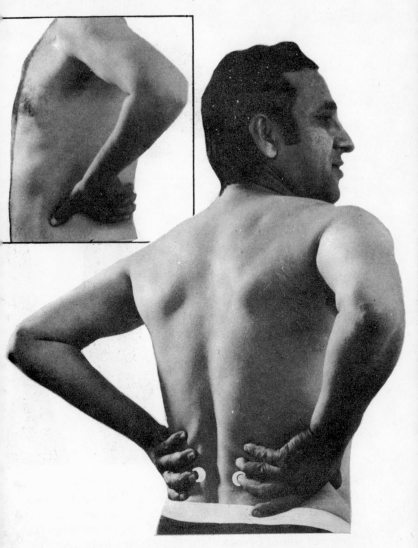

the side of the middle of the spinal column. Points are
located at the same level as the bottom of the rib cage.

*Fig. 9*
**Back Point 2** *(Trigger Points): Located by bending neck slightly and noting prominent vertebral bone protruding at the base of the neck. Counting it as one, count down five vertebral spines (spines of the back bone). In between the fifth and the sixth spine and two fingerbreadths to each side of the centre of the backbone lie the points.*

28

## Low Back Pain

Back point 3 (fig. 10) even in these relatively permissive times it is awkward to press or massage in public. It also may not be overly effective for everyone but is an important point for low back pain.

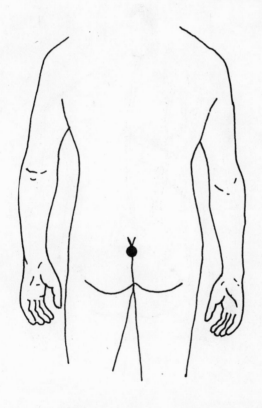

*Fig. 10*
**Back Point 3** *(Governing Vessel 1 and 2): Located just beneath the tip of the tail bone.*

## Sciatica

Back point 4 (fig. 11) which technically is about three quarters of an inch in back of the hip joint obviously lies deep under the skin, and to stimulate it requires a fair degree of pressure and massage. This particular point is especially beneficial for sciatica, but is also very useful bilaterally for low back pain.

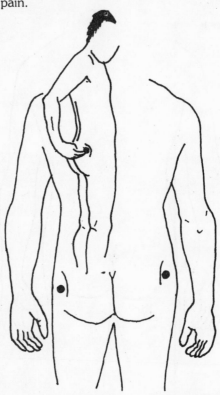

Fig. 11
**Back Point 4** (Gall Bladder 30): *Located by standing slightly on tip toes and noting the depression formed at the sides of the buttocks. The point is located in the centre of the depression or ring.*

Another deep point is back point 5 (fig. 12) which can be used bilaterally. Again, unless the site is unusually tender (a general rule) deep strong pressure, rotating the finger when useful, is required.

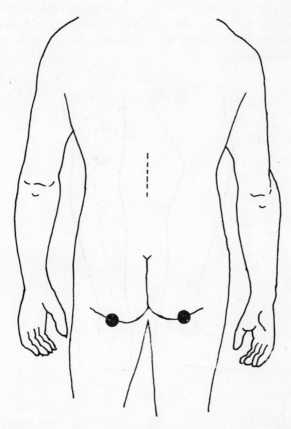

Fig. 12
**Back Point 5** *(Bladder 51) : Located at the midpoint of the crease the lower end of the buttocks makes with the thigh.*

## Sciatica, Muscle Spasms and Tired Legs

Knee point 4, (fig. 13), leg point 2, (fig. 14) and ankle-foot point 5 (fig. 15) are also effective points in low back pain, even though they are extremity points. They should be used bilaterally (on both sides). It is still a mystery why points remote from the injury are useful in acupuncture, and many yet unproven theories abound to try to explain it. However, we do not always need to understand a benefit in order to take advantage of it.

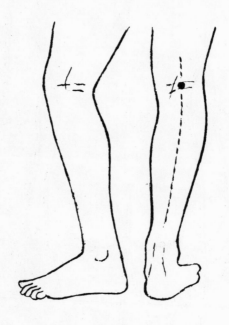

*Fig. 13*
**Knee Point 4** *(Bladder 54) : Located on the back portion of the knee exactly at the midpoint of the crease. See also Fig. 30.*

To be used bilaterally for low back pain.

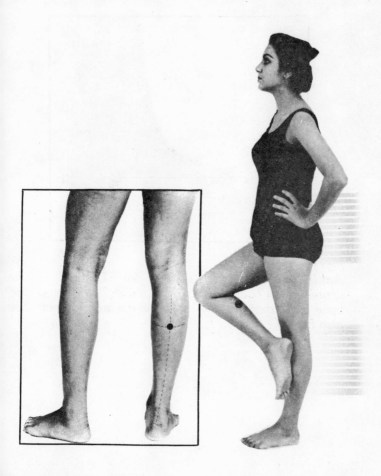

*Fig. 14*
**Leg Point 2** *(Bladder 57): At the lower tip of the calf muscle in the vertical midline of the back of the leg. (Roughly in the centre of the back of the leg).*

Again use ankle-foot point 5 bilaterally for this indication.

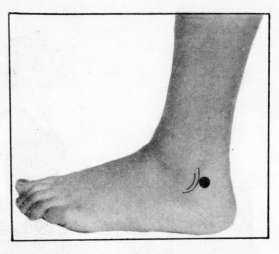

Fig. 15
**Ankle-foot Point 5** (Bladder 60): Located in the depression in back of the lateral malleolus, (the rounded bone protruding from the ankle on the outer aspect). See also Fig. 38.

# 5

## Wrist Ailments

The wrist is injured in all sports as are the fingers. The wrist is very responsive to acupressure or pressure acupuncture. There are a number of important points in this area which besides having use in wrist arthritis or sprains are used for illnesses quite remote from them and for general systemic problems. The figures will be repeated when these illnesses are discussed, but for now the wrist itself is the object of our attention. Wrist-hand point 1 is described in figure 16. Pressure can be used with or without massage.

### Wrist Injuries

Wrist-hand point 2 (fig. 17) is an important point for wrist injuries. It can be used either with pressure alone or with rotation of the finger. The applications should be for several minutes at a time and more than one point can be stimulated simultaneously. Of course, if the injured party is working on himself, the uninjured hand works on the injured. If both hands or wrists are involved, he may need help.

Fig. 16
**Wrist-hand Point 1** (Lung 7) : Located on the thumb side
of the wrist just above the radial tuberosity (a projection of
bone just above the thumb side of the wrist). It can be found
by placing the hands as shown in the illustration. It is about
two fingerbreadths above the wrist fold. See also Figs. 64
& 88.

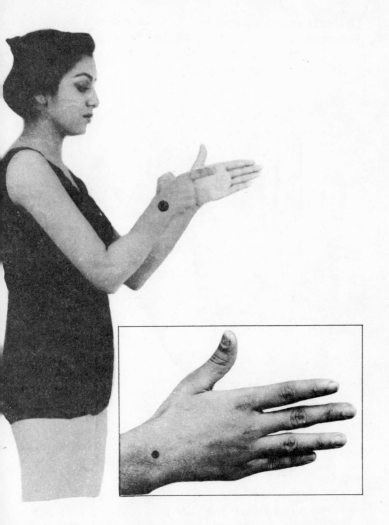

Fig. 17
**Wrist-hand Point 2** (Tripple Burner 4): Located on the
back of the wrist at about the middle of the wrist at the
flexion crease.

37

This point, wrist-hand point 3 (fig. 18) is one of those points that has important uses other than for wrist injuries. It is a fair help in wrist ailments and should be employed especially if the injury's pain makes it difficult to relax at night.

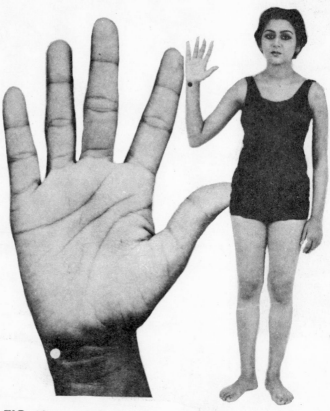

FIG. 18
**Wrist-hand Point 3** (Heart 7): Located on the palmar aspect of the wrist at the first crease after the hand-wrist junction crease on the little finger side of the hand. (Seven eights of the width of the wrist from the thumb side). See also Figs. 75 & 95.

Wrist-hand point 4 is another important point for the wrist alone. It can be handled like the one on its opposite side (wrist-hand point 2) and the thumb and index or middle finger of the uninjured hand can simultaneously be applied to the two points

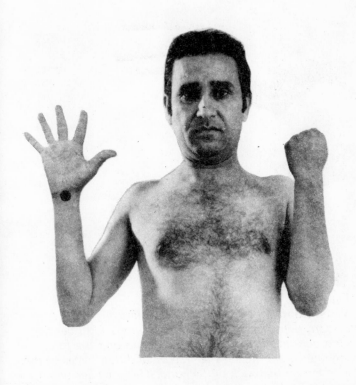

Fig. 19
**Wrist-hand Point 4** (Pericardium 7): Located at the centre of the hand-wrist junction crease on the palmar side.

Wrist-hand point 5 is one of the most important points in the body. It is very useful in wrist trauma, and pressure alone will probably be the most effective method of using it even though rotation can be tried. In the treatment of systemic

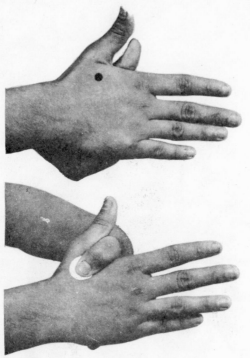

Fig. 20

**Wrist-hand Point 5** (Large Intestine 4): It is located midway between the two bones of thumbs and index finger. One can find it by closing the thumb and the forefinger together and noticing the little mound that forms at their junction on the back of the hand. The point lies under the peak of the little mound. It can also be found by bending the thumb of the other hand over the web between the thumb and the index finger as shown in the illustration. It lies under the end of the thumb. See also Figs. 63, 69, 76, 82 & 92.

40

injuries more pressure usually can be tolerated than in treating a local injury, since the local injury, naturally, has local pain near the site. But as the condition improves increased pressure can be tolerated for local injuries.

## Finger Injuries and Finger Arthritis

It must also be kept in mind with fresh injuries that fractures can be part of the trauma, and in those cases where the pain is unusually severe it is imperative that x-rays be obtained before instituting pressure acupuncture. Wrist-hand point 6 (fig. 21) has more use in finger injuries and finger arthritis.

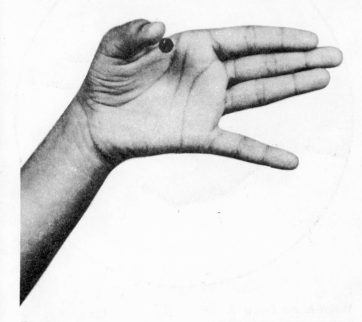

Fig. 21
**Wrist-hand Point 6** *(Large intestine 3) : Located under the thumb side of the index finger one fingerbreadth below the base of the finger at the mid point of the side of the hand.*

41

## Trauma and Arthritis of the Fingers

The next three points, wrist hand points 7, 8, and 9 (figs. 22, 23 and 24) have uses other than local, but they are useful in trauma and arthritis of the fingers. As a general rule for local ailments the closer a key (important) acupuncture site, is to the area of injury, the more effect it will have, but all the points should be tried.

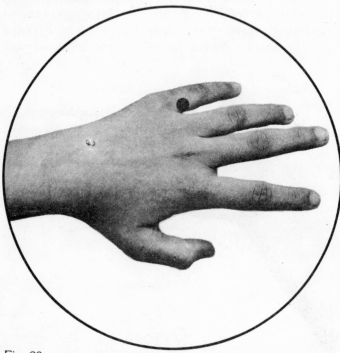

Fig. 22
**Wrist-hand Point 7** (Tripple Burner 2): Located in the web between the little finger and the ring finger on the back side. Wrist-hand Point 7 should be pressed at a 45⁰ angle toward the hand, the point being approached from the top of the hand.

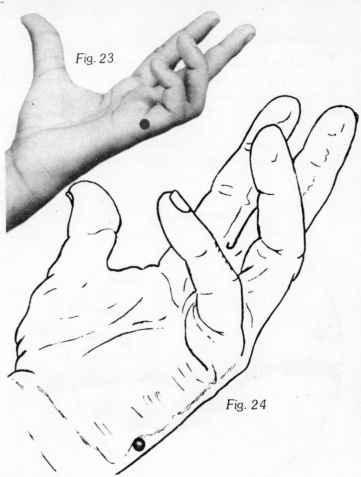

Fig. 23

**Wrist-hand Point 8** *(Small intestine 3)* : Located on the side of the hand one fingerbreadth above the base of the little finger.

Fig. 24

**Wrist-hand Point 9** *(Small intestine 4)* : Located under the side of the hand two fingerbreadths above wirst point 8.

## Forearm Pain

The next two points, wrist-hand 10 and wrist-hand 11 (figs. 25 and 26) have an important use in acupuncture anesthesia, since these points are used in chest operations, including open heart surgery and lung resections, unbelieveable as it may be. However, no one here is suggesting that such a use should be applied at this time. They are useful in wrist and forearm pain, nevertheless.

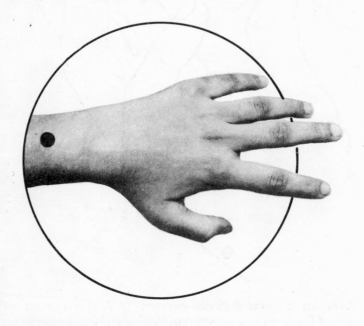

FIG. 25
**Wrist-hand Point 10** (Tripple Burner 5): Located on the back side of the forearm three fingerbreadths from the middle of the wrist crease. See also Fig. 96.

The two points can be pressed simultaneously by the middle or index finger and the thumb. Straight pressure or pressure with rotation can be used. Since these points are remote from the wrist itself, in the common sprained wrist, they can be pressed harder than the otherwise more effective previously described points and thus have their value enhanced.

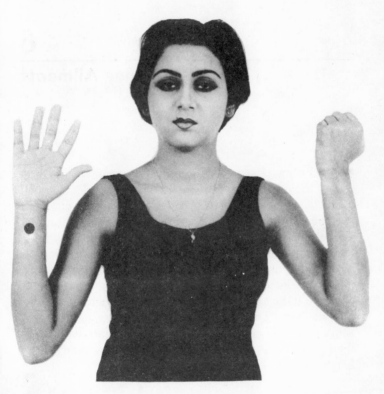

Fig. 26
**Wrist-hand Point 11** (Pericardium 6): Located on the palm side of the forearm three fingerbreadths from the middle of the wrist crease. See also Fig. 51.

# 6

## Knee Ailments

The knee is a part of the body that can go wrong easily in athletic endeavours. Unfortunately, serious ligamentous tears and torn cartilages can result from seemingly insignificant, as well as significant trauma. Therefore, it is important to see a doctor about any knee that seems seriously injured before relying too much on pressure acupuncture.If the doctor feels conservative therapy is indicated then acupressure should be given a good try. If the knee does not respond, the doctor should be re-consulted. This advice actually applies to pressure acupuncture in general but is more important with some things than others. The first knee point is knee point 1, (fig. 27).

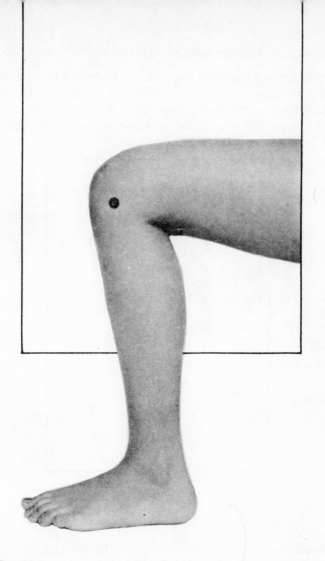

Fig. 27
**Knee Point 1** (Stomach 35): Location can be seen by
slightly bending the knee and finding the depression at the
lower outside edge of the knee cap.

## Knee/Leg injuries and Knee Arthritis

Knee point 2 (fig. 28) is important with knee and leg injuries and arthritis of the knee. Since this point is usually somewhat remote to the actual injury, fairly strong pressure can be applied to it as well as rotational motion, if desired.

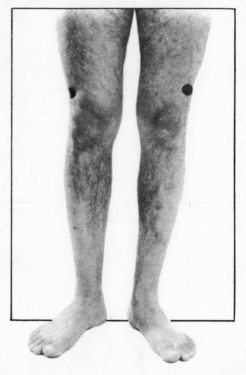

*Fig. 28*
***Knee Point 2*** *(Stomach 34) : It is located in the muscle that runs on the outside of the thigh, two inches up from the knee-cap. Have the patient sit on a chair and bend his leg at a 90⁰ angle. Measure two inches up from the top of the knee-cap. The point is slightly to the outside of the leg.*

Knee point 3 (fig. 29) is a point that has some other uses besides for knee injuries, but it is a point that should be included for pressure and massage in knee injuries and infirmities.

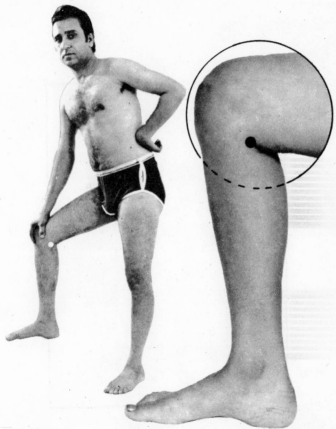

Fig. 29
**Knee Point 3** (Liver 8) : Location can be found by bending the knee and finding the crease formed on the medial or inner aspect. The point is at the end of the crease. See also Fig. 56.

Knee point 4 (fig. 30) has been previously encountered in back injuries. It also has its uses as a local point in knee injuries and is a very useful site. Pressure is especially helpful. Massage can be tried to see if it is of aid.

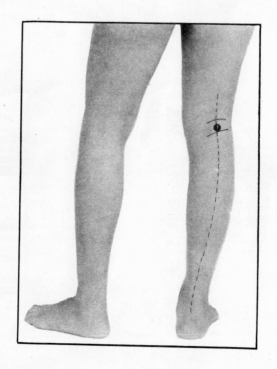

Fig. 30
**Knee Point 4** *(Bladder 54) : Located on the back portion of the knee exactly at the mid point of the crease. See also Fig. 13.*

Knee point 5 (fig. 31) is another general point as well as a local one. Again, it can be useful because it will frequently be away from the site of the injury and heavier pressure earlier can be applied here.

Knee point 6 (fig. 32) is another multiple use point that is somewhat removed from the usual sore point or injury point. It must also be remembered that occasionally these slightly remote points will be the object of injury, and then

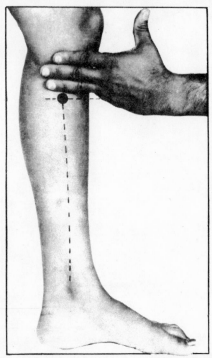

Fig. 31

**Knee Point 5** (Spleen 9): *Located at the top of the shinbone, on the inside of the leg. To make it simpler, it is located at a level three finger breadths below the lower level of the knee cap at the intersection of an imaginary line travelling vertically along the middle of the inside of the leg. See also Fig. 73.*

51

points closer to the knee itself can have pressure applied. Also, it is important to remember that the actual point of injury can be massaged gently at first in association with these pressure points being manipulated.

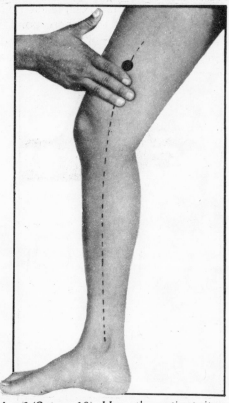

Fig. 32

**Knee Point 6** (Spleen 10) : *Have the patient sit and bend his leg at a 90° angle. Catch the centre of his knee-cap with the centre of your palm. The tip of your thumb will touch knee point 6, two inches above the knee-cap. In fact it is located at a level three finger breadths above the upper border of the knee cap where an imaginary line travelling vertically up the middle of the inside of the thigh crosses that level. See also Figs. 50 & 57.*

52

Knee point 7 (fig. 33) is another systemic site and has many uses. However, it is one of the most important points for knee disabilities, if not the most important, and should be considered first in the selection of what sites should be utilized

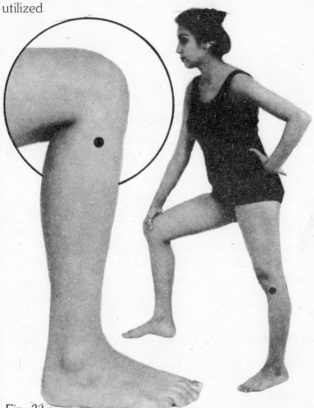

Fig. 33
**Knee Point 7** (Gall Bladder 34) : Located in front of and below the head of the fibula, which is the rounded knob located near the middle of the outside aspect of the leg at a level about two finger breadths below the lower level of the knee cap. The point itself is located in the depressed area in front of and below the fibula head. See also Fig. 83.

# 7

# Ankle-Foot Ailments

nkle-foot point 1 (fig. 34) is a very important point for ankle injuries, ankle edema and arthritis. It, usually, will be able to be pressed fairly hard and can stand rotation in the case of ankle injuries since the most painful parts of most ankle injuries are not at its proximity. If it is the only point that can be pressed and massaged, it is well worth while.

## Ankle Injuries, Ankle Edema and Arthritis

Ankle-foot point 2 (fig. 35) is another point that has great use in ankle infirmities. Unfortunately, it more frequently overlies a very tender point and must be pressed with care. Rotational massage can also be useful here if carefully initiated. Increasing the pressure if one is able to stand it.

Fig. 36 (ankle-foot point 3) and the following one, ankle-foot point 4 (fig. 37), can overlie tender parts of the foot when injured or ailing. These two points also have other uses in the acupuncture spectrum, which will be indicated later.

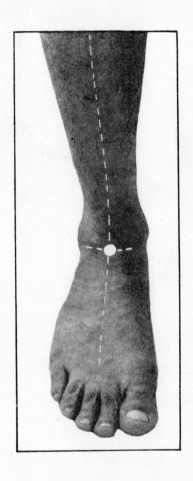

Fig. 34
**Ankle-foot Point 1** (Stomach 41) : Located in the centre of
the ankle crease as one flexes his ankle.

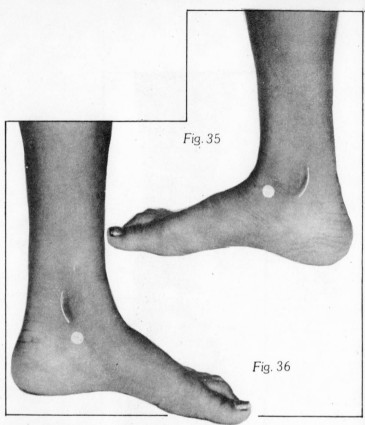

Fig. 35

**Ankle-foot Point 2** (Spleen 5): *Located directly in front of the lowest level of the medial malleolus or the middle ankle bone, (the rounded bone protruding from the ankle on the inner aspect).*

Fig. 36

**Ankle-foot Point 3** (Kidney 6): *Located one finger tip below the medical malleolus or the middle ankle bone, (the rounded bone protruding from the ankle on the inner aspect).*

Of the two ankle-foot points, point 3 has a greater use in the area of foot and ankle injuries, but ankle-foot point 4 which lies opposite to ankle-foot point 5 can be grasped along with ankle-foot point 5 (index finger on one and thumb on the other), and this area frequently is not a tender area.

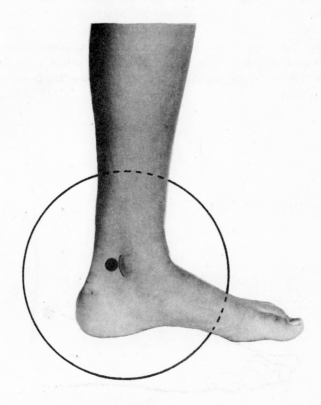

Fig. 37
**Ankle-foot Point 4** (Kidney 3): Located in the depression in back of the medial malleolus, (the rounded bone protruding from the ankle on the inner aspect).

Fig. 38, Previously shown as a back injury aid, ankle-foot point 5 is an important point in ankle injuries (as was said on the previous page, is often not in itself injured or at least not tender in ankle injuries). Firm pressure can frequently be applied.

Ankle-foot point 6 (fig. 39) is a unique point in which three of the Chinese meridians cross. So in actuality it overlies 3 acupuncture sites, or, in other words, it is three points in one. Needless to say it has many uses, one of which is an aid to ankle injuries. Since it is remote to the ankle it has the double advantage of usually being able to take firm pressure

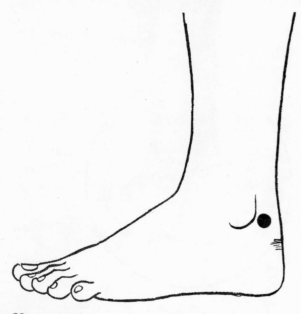

*Fig. 38*
**Ankle-foot Point 5** *(Bladder 60): Located in the depression in back of the lateral malleolus, (the rounded bone protruding from the ankle on the outer aspect). See also Fig. 15.*

and rotation. The point in the same position on the opposite side (lateral or outside of ankle) can be grasped and pressed simultaneously with ankle-foot point 6, if desired and if it proves helpful.

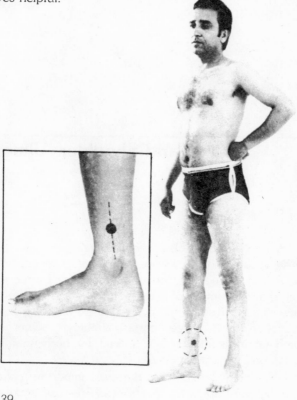

Fig. 39
**Ankle-foot Point 6** *(Spleen 6): Located four finger breadths above the medial malleolus or the inner rounded ankle bone at the middle of the inside aspect of the leg. Another easy way of locating this point is to flex the patient's foot and put his four fingers on the inside of his leg with the little finger resting on top of the anklebone and the other fingers going up the leg. Where the fourth finger lies, behind the shinbone, is spleen 6. See also Figs. 58, 72 & 81.*

# 8

# Neck and Shoulder Ailments

S houlder and neck injuries, while they are distinct and separate in many respects and can occur individually and frequently, too often together. Furthermore, they share a number of acupuncture sites. Therefore, it is convenient to discuss the two together. We will divide the discussion into three parts: shoulder points only, combination points (points shared by both anatomical parts), and neck points only.

Shoulder point 1 (fig. 40) is the most important point for relieving pure shoulder disabilities. Pressure and rotary massage may be used. The same is true for shoulder point 2 (fig. 41).

Shoulder point 3 (fig. 42) is also a point reserved for shoulder injuries and disabilities only. These three points can be used singly or together. As with the other parts previously described, the most pressure can be used over points more remote from the injury. All points should be used initially and then determination made if one point is superior to the

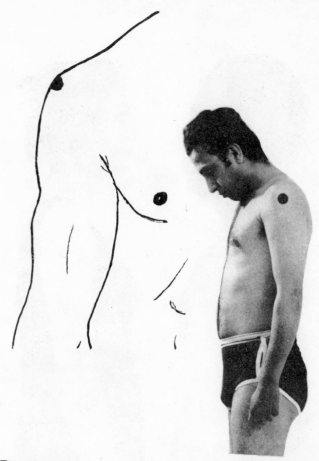

Fig. 40

**Shoulder Point 1** (*Large Intestine 15*): It is located on the outside of the shoulder bone. Have the patient raise his bent elbow to an angle of 90⁰ from the body. The indentation is easier to see. In short it is located at the midpoint of the top of the outside of the arm just below the end of the shoulder bone.

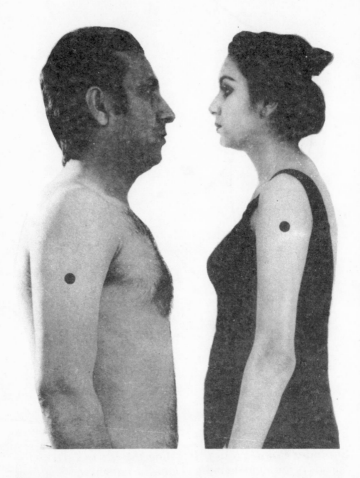

*Fig. 41*
**Shoulder Point 2** *(Large Intestine 14): Located at the midpoint of the outside of the arm (upper arm) where the tip of the (upside down appearing) triangular deltoid muscle is.*

others, since some of the combination points also should be used. In cases such as the shoulder where up to 6 or 7 sites are available, it is not always possible let alone convenient to use all.

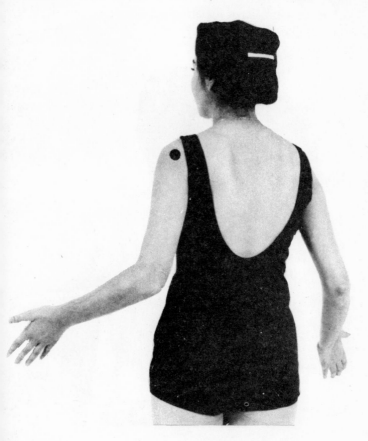

Fig. 42
**Shoulder Point 3** (Tripple Burner 14): Located on the back of the shoulder above the arm pit, in the soft tissue just below the bony top of the shoulder.

These next series of points have less direct action on the upper arm or outside portion of the shoulder. However, they do help and are very beneficial for the inside portion of the shoulder which includes the upper shoulder blade are a and the upper axilla or the armpit. Shoulder point 4 (fig. 43) is of more help to the shoulder than the neck but is of value to both.

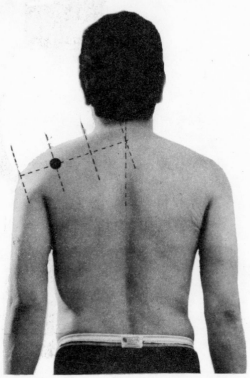

Fig. 43
**Shoulder Point 4** (Small Intestine 12): Located on an imaginary line drawn from the tip of the shoulder to a point lying over the middle of the base of the back of the neck. The point is one third along that line from the shoulder.

## Neck Injuries and Arthritis

Shoulder point 5 (fig. 44) becomes a point that is very useful in neck injuries and arthritis, but it also has a very beneficial use in tension headaches and tension in the neck. The succeeding points also will have good use in these conditions. Shoulder point 5 also can be used for shoulder injuries. Pressure and massage is good for all of these combination points, and for the neck they should be treated bilaterally.

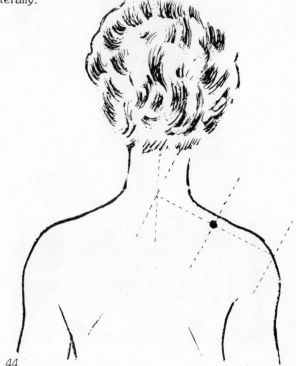

*Fig. 44*
**Shoulder Point 5** *(Gall Bladder 21): Located on an imaginary line drawn from the tip of the shoulder to a point lying over the middle of the base of the back of the neck. The point is on the mid piont of that line.*

Shoulder point 6 (fig. 45) is the combination point more valuable for neck problems than shoulder problems, although it can be used for both. The use of trigger points is especially valuable in this area. The trigger point is the point frequently away from the acupuncture site that is tender and painful. It should also be pressed and massaged along with the acupuncture sites.

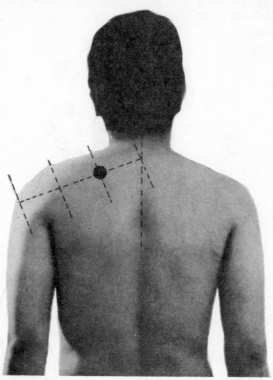

Fig. 45
**Shoulder Point 6** (Small Intestine 15): Located on an imaginary line drawn from the tip of the shoulder to a point lying over the middle of the base of the back of the neck. The point is one third along that line from the neck.

Neck point 2 (fig. 46) is a key point for neck injuries and arthritic pains, tension headaches and many other ailments. It is found by bending the head forward, but it is better stimulated in most cases by keeping the head upright. Pressure and rotary massage both can be used.

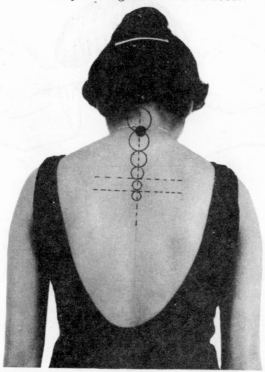

Fig. 46

**Neck Point 2** (*Governing Vessel 14*) : *This point is located between seventh cervical vertebra and first thoracic vertibra. To make it simple it can be detected by bending the neck slightly and noting prominent bone at base of neck. Point is located just below this prominent vertebral spine in the space in between it and the next lower (and less prominent) vertebral or back bone spine. See also Fig. 89*

Neck point 3 (fig. 47) is used bilaterally as are all points beneficial to the neck, except, or course, those overlying the spine. This point will be covered again when anxiety is discussed.

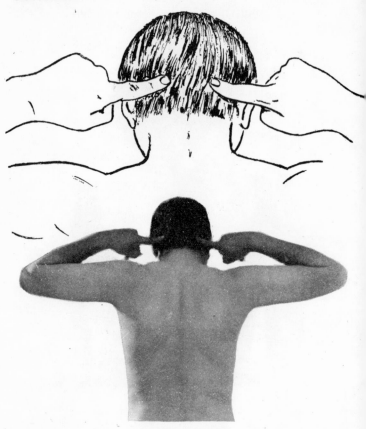

Fig. 47
**Neck Point 3** (Bladder 10) : This point is located just below the first cervical vertebra located on each side of the spine at the natural level of the hair line, each point being one fingerbreadth to the side of the spine. See also Fig. 84.

# 9
## Obesity

**P**erhaps the most aggravating condition that people must suffer from in day to day living is the inability to maintain desirable body weight. Most of the time overweight is the problem and dieting and taking diet pills is the way of life for millions. Using acupuncture sites is a recent entry into this area and is presently the subject of research. With needles there has been an initial success with some extremely difficult patients. Using the technique of pressure acupuncture also has proved promising in my practice. Abdomen point 1 (fig. 48) on the left side overlies the stomach. It must be pressed deeply. Massage is not necessary.

Leg point 1 (fig. 49) also can be used on both legs or on one leg. If using two is too cumbersome one works well enough. In general, the way obesity points should be utilized is at the time one feels hungry. The most effective points should be pressed for several minutes. The ones that work best must be discovered for each individual by himself by trial and error.

Fig. 48

**Abdomen Point 1** *(Stomach 21) : Located by placing the fingers of the left hand together and straight, then placing the tip of the index finger by the umbilicus—just below the web between the ring finger and little finger lies the point.*

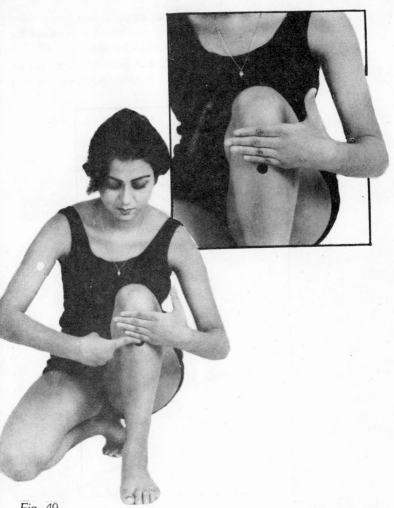

Fig. 49
**Leg Point 1** (Stomach 36): Located four fingerbreadths below the lower level of the knee cap and about one fingerbreadth to the outside of the shin bone in the soft tissue there.

Knee point 6 (fig. 50) is another point that can be used unilaterally or bilaterally. It may not be as successful for most people as the previous points. The same may be true for wrist hand point 11 (fig. 51) but both of these points should be given a good try. I have mentioned that the points

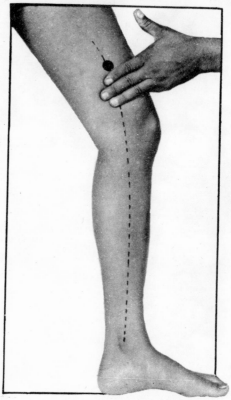

Fig. 50

**Knee Point 6** (Spleen 10): *Located at a level three fingerbreadths above the upper border of the knee cap where an imaginary line travelling vertically up the middle of the inner thigh crosses that level. See also Figs. 32 & 57.*

should be pressed for a few minutes. Actually up to ten minutes for a meal or a hunger period may be more advantageous.

Unfortunately obese persons frequently lack the will power to do anything that controls appetite, and if they don't spend a reasonable period pressing the points, the points, of course, will not help.

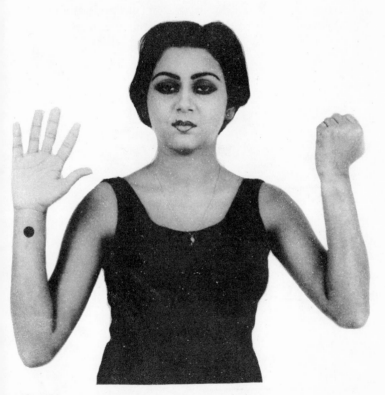

Fig. 51
**Wrist-hand Point 11** (Pericardium 6): *Located on the palm side of the forearm three fingerbreadths above the middle of the wrist crease. See also Fig. 26.*

## For Curbing the Appetite

Acupuncture sites on the ears are also beneficial in curbing the appetite, and while it may be awkward to stick your fingers in your ears in public when eating out, it can be used at home. Figures 52 and 53 demonstrate these points. Simply place the index fingers into the ears as shown, pressing over the site. A fair amount of pressure should be used even if it is a little unpleasant. If done properly and persistently it will reduce hunger in many people.

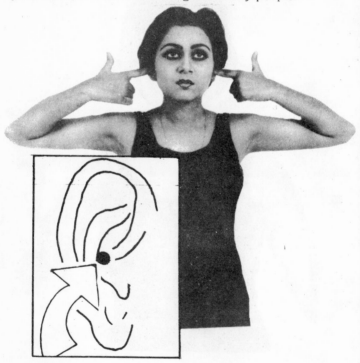

*Fig. 52 & 53*
***Ear Point 1*** *(Pericardium 6): Follow the rim of the ear around until it ends up in front by becoming the ridge within the ear itself. The point lies immediately behind the end of the ridge.*

# 10

## Impotence

I mpotence is another very frustrating experience for men, and for women in their relationship with men. Pressure and massage on the acupuncture sites can be beneficial. It can be of even greater value if the person afflicted remains calm and his partner uses restraint in criticising or showing contempt even by facial expressions. Fig. 54 is a key point. Pressure against it with rotary massage can be used by either partner.

Back point 2 (fig. 55), knee point 3 (fig. 56), knee point 6 (fig. 57), ankle-foot point 6 (fig. 58) and abdomen point 4 (fig. 59) are all useful points and should all be tried. Those points that are bilateral should be used bilaterally. Pressure and massage can both be used. Apply strong pressure except where a point may be particularly sensitive.

One must not give up easily in this endeavour, and if initially there is lack of success, a rest period in order with relaxing, light conversation and no recriminations is always beneficial. Then one should make try at another points.

The most effort and time should be directed at the points illustrated in figures 54, 55, and 59, but the other should be tried too.

Fig. 54
**Penis Point** (Trigger point) : Located in the mid point of the base of the penis at its junction with the scrotum.

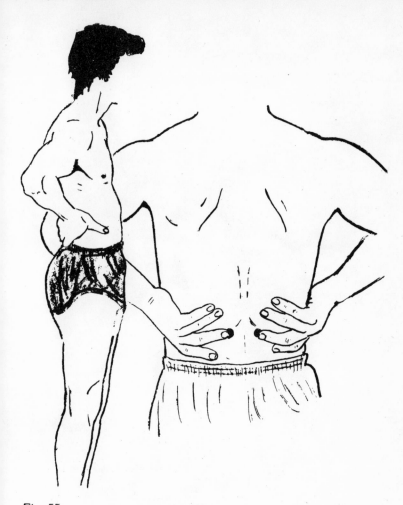

Fig. 55
**Back Point 2** *(Bladder 23) : Located between second and third lumber vertebrae, just behind the navel on each side of the . spinal column, each point lying about two finger-breadths to the side of the middle of the spinal column. Points are located at the same level as the bottom of the rib cage. See also Fig. 8.*

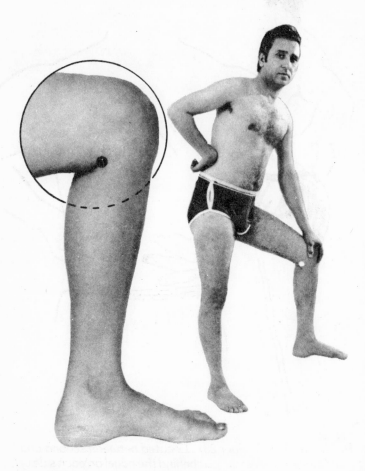

Fig. 56
**Knee Point 3** *(Liver 8)* : Located by bending the knee and
finding the crease formed on the medial or inner aspect.
The point is at the end of the crease. See also Fig. 29.

Ten or even fifteen minutes should be devoted to the acupuncture sites. At that point an attempt at the conventional type of love play or stimulation should be made. It must be kept in mind that pressure acupuncture is not a form of love play, but it is a therapeutic effort to restore the proper balance in the nervous system so that an erection can take place.

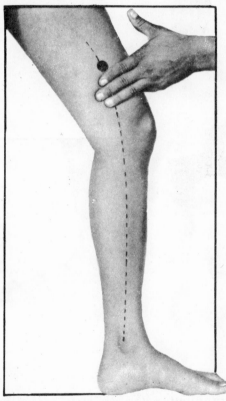

Fig. 57
**Knee Point 6** (Spleen 10) : Located at a level three fingerbreadths above the level of the upper border of the knee cap where an imaginary line travelling vertically up the middle of the thigh crosses that level. See also Figs. 32 & 50.

Pressure on these indicated points is not in itself a form of sex. It is used so that the conventional forms of sex which are not working at the time will start to work. Therefore, if the acupressure does not in itself produce an erection it is not necessarily designed to do that.

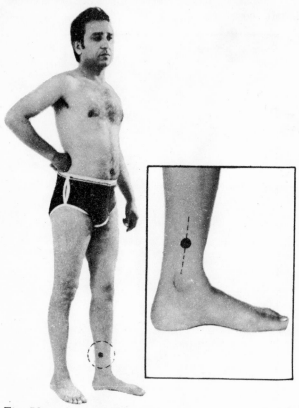

Fig. 58
**Ankle-foot Point 6** (Spleen 6) : Located four finger-breadths above the medial malleolus or the inner rounded ankle bone at the middle of the inside aspect of the leg. See also Figs. 39, 72, & 81.

Acupressure is designed to enable the person to obtain an erection when those things that formerly produced an erection are again induced. One must not give up easily and get discouraged. Especially, one must have a positive attitude toward solving the problem.

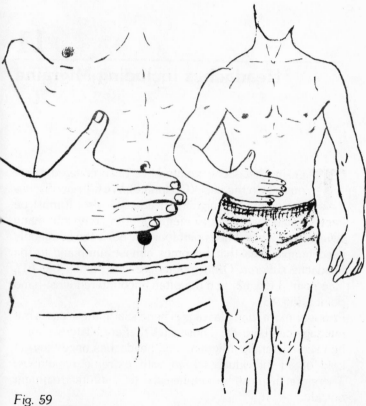

Fig. 59
**Abdomen Point 4** (Conception Vessel 4) : Located in the middle of the abdomen, one and a half inches below the navel or four fingerbreadths below the umbilicus. See also Fig. 80.

# 11

## Headaches including Migraine

Tension headache points have been covered previously with the neck (Chapter 8). We will now discuss the points for migraine headaches also. It must be kept in mind that some elements of both creep into many severe headaches. Face point four (fig. 60) is the commonly used temple area that becomes almost automatic to the headache sufferer. Other points are face point 1 (fig. 61), face point 3 (fig. 62) and the often encountered wrist-hand point 5 (fig. 63).

Pressure more than massage is beneficial in these cases but massage can be tried. Those sites that are bilateral should be used bilaterally. Migraine and headaches, once they get hold of an individual, let go with extreme reluctance. Therefore, it must be emphasized to institute treatment quickly.

If the headaches are severe enough much effort must be taken to obtain relief. Help by a friend to press the wrist-hand sites (figs. 63 and 64) while you press the face points is

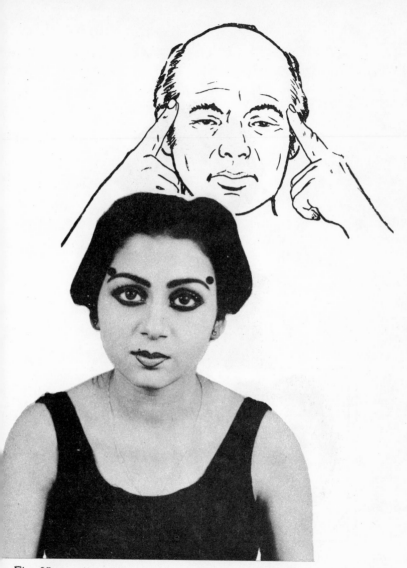

Fig. 60
**Face Point 4** (Sun X) : Located on each side of the
forehead one fingerbreadth lateral to the eyebrow in the
temple area. See also Fig. 77.

83

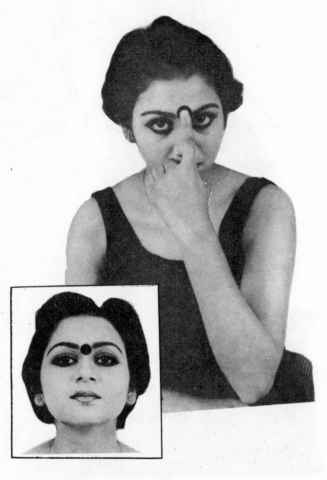

Fig. 61
**Face Point 1** (Governing Vessel 24.5) : Located on the
center of the forehead midway between the eyebrows.

useful. Medication prescribed by a doctor may be necessary, but in any case pressure acupuncture can be of enormous help either as the prime treatment or as an adjunct.

Fig. 62

**Face Point 3** *(Tripple Burner 23) : Located on each side of the forehead at the outer edge of the eyebrows. See also Fig. 99.*

Keep in mind to massage and put pressure on the neck points and the trigger points also, especially if the pain is in back. Pressing the trigger points as well as the acupuncture sites helps. (A trigger point is any point that is tender. In the neck it is usually due to muscle spasm).

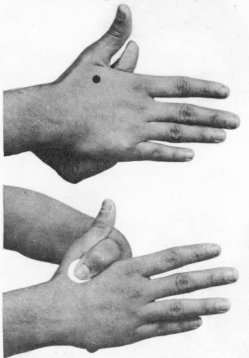

Fig. 63
**Wrist-hand Point 5** *(Large Intestine 4) : It is located between the two bones of thumbs and index finger. One can find it by closing the thumb and the forefinger together and noticing the little mound that forms at their junction on the back of the hand. The point lies at the peak of the little mound. It can also be found by bending the thumb of the other hand over the web between the thumb and the index finger as shown in the illustration. It lies under the end of the thumb. See also Figs. 20, 69, 76, 82 & 92.*

Another point, wrist-hand point 1 (fig. 64) is useful generally in headaches of any origin.

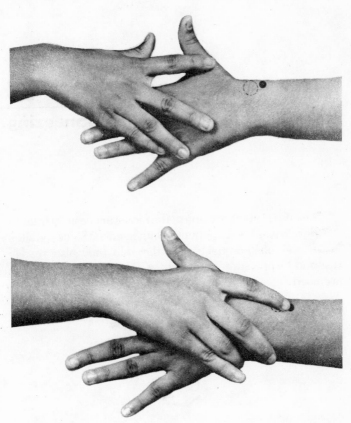

Fig. 64
**Wrist-hand Point 1** *(Lung 7) : Located on the thumb side of the wrist just above the radial tuberosity (a projection of bone just above the thumb side of the wrist). Can be found by placing the hands as shown in the illustration. It is about two fingerbreadths above the wrist fold. See also Figs. 16 & 88.*

# 12

# Sinus Trouble and Sneezing

Sinus troubles are one of the most successfully treated illnesses by acupuncture with needles. Since the sites are located just under the skin they also readily respond to pressure acupuncture. Pressure plus massage are used.

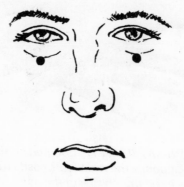

Fig. 65
**Face Point 6** *(Stomach 2)* : *Located under the pupil of each eye just below the lower border of the eye socket.*

The sites are face point 6 (fig. 65), face point 2 (fig. 66), and face point 7 (fig. 67). A few minutes on each bilateral site several times a day should produce good results within two weeks.

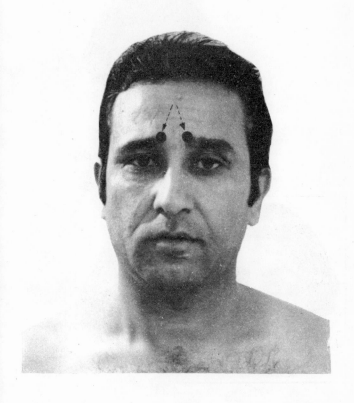

Fig. 66
**Face Point 2** *(Bladder 2) : Located on each side of the forehead at the middle edge of the eyebrows.*

Maintenance therapy should be used after that, especially in times when the victim is exposed to allergic conditions such as pollens, smog and any other irritant he may be aware of.

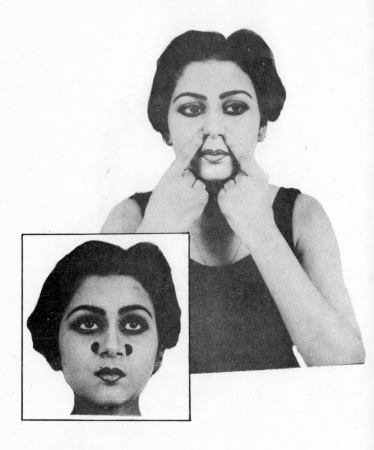

Fig. 67
**Face Point 7** (*Large Intestine 20*) : *Located just to the side of the base of the nose on each side.*

## Nose Bleeding and Sneezing

Face point 9 (fig. 68) is useful to stop nose bleeds and to stifle a sneeze. Firm pressure without massage is the best method of application. To stifle a sneeze face point 9 can be used alone or in conjunction with face point 10 (Fig. 98):

Fig. 68
**Face Point 9** (Governing Vessel 25): Located over the centre of the nose just above the tip.

# 13

## Toothaches

**T**oothaches can be helped by needle acupuncture. If one should get one in the middle of the night it certainly is worth trying pressure acupuncture if aspirin does not work. Wrist-hand point 5 (fig. 69) is

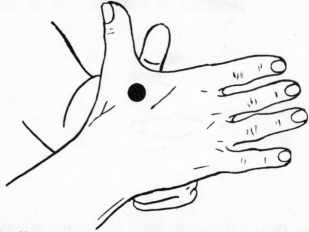

Fig. 69
**Wrist-hand Point 5** (Large Intestine 4) : Located by closing the thumb and the forefinger together and noticing

frequently effective by itself. It should be primarily tried on the toothache side, but if it does not work, the other side can be used also.

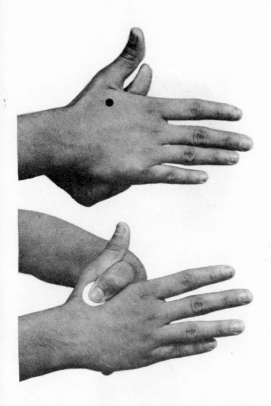

the little mound that forms at their junction on the back of the hand. The point lies under the peak of the little mound. It can also be found by bending the thumb of the other hand over the web between the thumb and the index finger as shown in the illustration. It lies under the end of the thumb. See also Figs. 20, 63, 76, 82 & 92.

Face point 8 (fig. 70) and face point 5 (fig. 71) are other points used, but unfortunately these might be quite tender. The non-affected side can be tried, but the use of both sides is not more effective, as a rule, than the involved side.

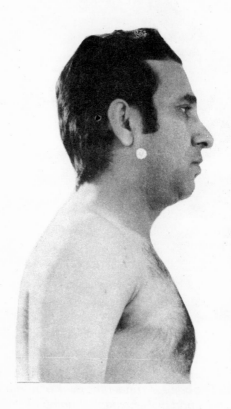

Fig. 70
**Face Point 8** (Stomach 6) : Located on each side of the face just above the point that the angle of the jaw makes.

However, wrist-hand point 5 by itself, unilaterally or bilaterally, is very effective. Hard pressure should be used. Of course, one should see a dentist as soon as possible to get the condition corrected.

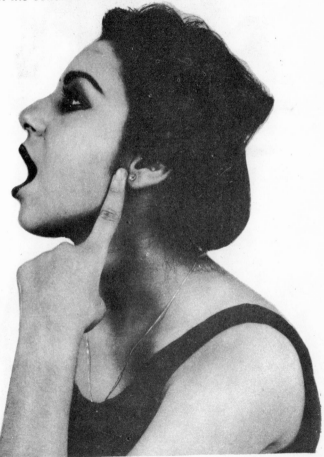

Fig. 71
**Face Point 5** *(Gall Bladder 2)* : *Located on each side of the face by opening the mouth wide and feeling the depression*

formed in front of the ears at the top of the ear lobe level.
Pressure should be applied with mouth closed. See also Fig.
101.

# 14

## Menstrual Difficulties

**M**enstrual difficulties are a plague for many women whether it is the agony of premenstrual tension or the inconvenience of excess or irregular flow. These conditions should be diagnosed by a gynecologist or family doctor in any case, but either as a primary treatment or adjunct treatment, pressure on acupuncture sites can be useful. The first point is ankle-foot point 6 (fig. 72).

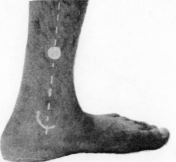

*Fig. 72*
**Ankle-foot Point 6** *(Spleen 6) : Located four finger-breadths above the medial malleolus or the inner rounded ankle bone at the middle of the inside aspect of the leg. See also Figs. 39, 58 & 81.*

Additional points for menstrual difficulties are knee point 5 (fig. 73) and abdomen point 3 (fig. 74). Bilateral points should be pressed and massaged on both sides.

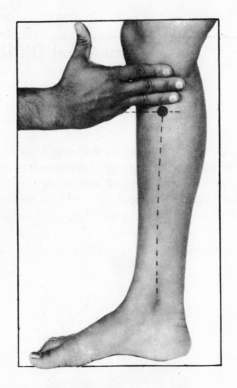

*Fig. 73*
**Knee Point 5** *(Spleen 9) : Located at a level three fingerbreadths below the lower level of the knee cap at the intersection of an imaginary line travelling vertically along the middle of the inside of the leg. See also Fig. 31.*

If one is prone to pre-menstrual tension it is wise to start therapy several days before the period is supposed to start and continue it for several days after. If one has heavy flow it is best to start the therapy on the first day of the cycle and continue it until the period stops. If one gets intermittent flow through the month, apply the treatment daily.

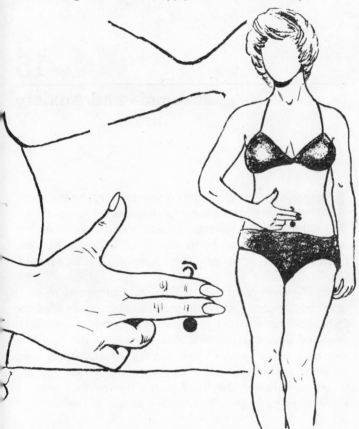

*Fig. 74*
**Abdomen Point 3** *(Conception Vessel 6) : Located two fingerbreadths below the umbilicus.*

# 15

## Insomnia and Anxiety

Insomnia is a problem that confronts everyone from time to time. For some it is a completely agonizing experience requiring heavy reliance on sedatives. Pressure on the acupuncture sites can be benefit. The sites are wrist-hand point 3 (fig. 75), wrist-hand point 5 (fig. 76) and face point 4 (fig. 77).

Since the wrist-hand points lie in close proximity to each other both points can be pressed simultaneously. Use the thumb on the wrist-hand point 5 and the index or middle finger on wrist-hand point 3. Also the same wrist-hand site can be pressed on each side simultaneously. Apply hard pressure for several minutes, then relax. When you are weary of pressing the hand points try the face point 4 bilaterally which you will recognize as one of the migraine points.

Diligence and frequent application while you are trying to sleep will often allow you to drift off. Remember, at that time you have nothing else to do. Press the points and count sheep, and before you know it you will be asleep.

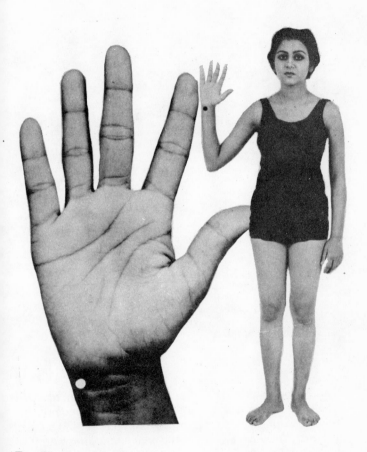

Fig. 75
**Wrist-hand Point 3** (Heart 7) : Located on the palmar
aspect of the wrist at the first crease after the hand-wrist in
the little finger side of the hand. (Seven eights of the width of
the wrist from the thumb side). See also Figs. 18 & 95.

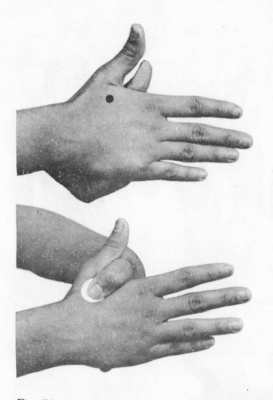

Fig. 76

**Wrist-hand Point 5** (*Large Intestine 4*) : *Located by closing the thumb and the forefinger together and noticing the little mound that forms at their junction on the back of the hand. The point lies under the peak of the little mound. It can also be found by bending the thumb of the other hand over the web between the thumb and the index finger as shown in the illustration. The point lies under the end of the thumb. End of thumb is directly on site. See also Figs. 20, 63, 69, 82 & 92.*

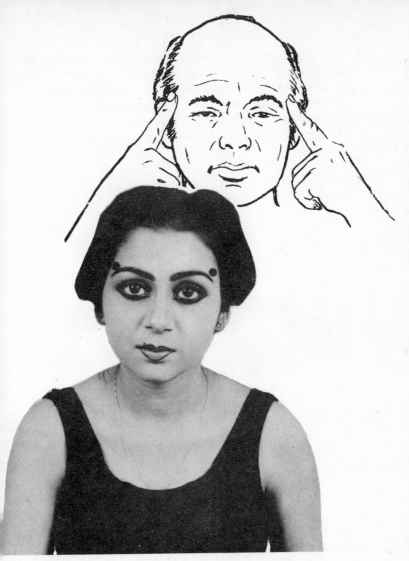

Fig. 77
**Face Point 4** (Sun X) : Located on each side of the head
one fingerbreadth lateral to the eyebrow in the temple area.
See also Fig. 60.

Neck point 3 (fig. 78) pressed bilaterally with massage plus the three preceding points, especially wrist-hand point 3 (fig. 75) and wrist-hand point 5 (fig. 76), are useful to help relieve anxiety. Tranquilizers and anti-depressants may also be indicated and psychiatric treatment in extreme cases; so, consult your physician if this is a persistent and unrelieved condition.

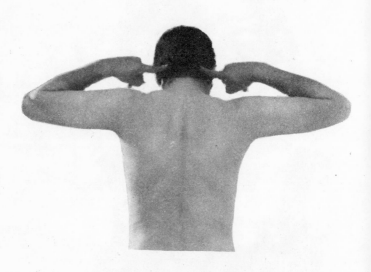

Fig. 78
**Neck Point 3** (Bladder 10) : Just below the first cervical vertebra is located on each side of the spine at the natural level of the hair line, each point being one fingerbreadth to the side of the spine. Site is directly under tip of Index finger. See also Fig. 47

# 16

# Sore Throat and Wind Pipe Irritation

This point is useful not only in general coughing, but especially if you happen to inhale bits of liquid such as saliva or anything you are drinking. We used to call it getting something down your Sunday throat. Anyway, light to medium pressure over neck point 1 (fig. 79) can sometimes stop a non-productive cough and help you not embarrass yourself in a theatre, library or a place where you are supposed to be silent.

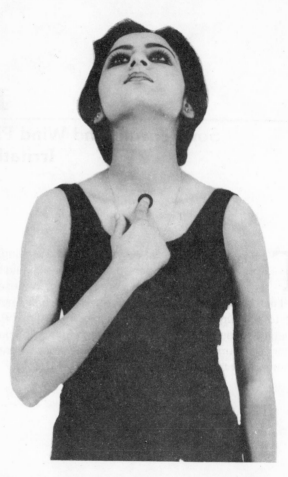

Fig. 79
**Neck Point 1** (Conception Vessel 22) : Located just above
the sternal notch or just above the breast bone where the
soft tissue of the front of the neck begins. Site is directly
under tip of Index finger. See also Fig. 91.

# 17

## Abdominal Pain

T his type of pain requires the consultation of a doctor. But while waiting for him to arrive or with his approval after a diagnosis has been made, acupuncture points which help relieve abdominal pain will be identified.

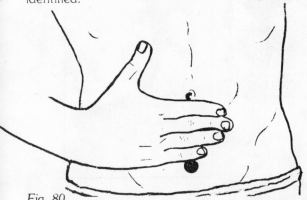

Fig. 80

**Abdomen Point 4** (Conception Vessel 4) : Located in the middle of the abdomen, one and a half inches below the navel four fingerbreadths below the umbilicus. See also Fig. 59

Abdomen point 4 (fig. 80) and ankle-foot point 6 (fig. 81) (the menstrual cramp point) can be used for lower intestinal pain. The umbilicus, itself, is the acupuncture point for middle abdomen pain as well as the two points located 3 fingerbreadths to each side of it. Pressure can be hard over extremity sites, but over the abdomen itself pressure over a very tender site must not be applied. Pick points remote from areas of acute tenderness.

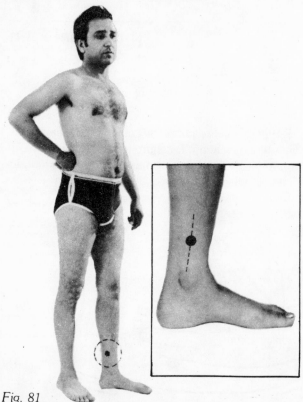

*Fig. 81*
**Ankle-foot Point 6** *(Spleen 6) : Located four finger-breadths above the medial malleolus or the inner rounded ankle bone at the middle of the inside aspect of the leg. See also Figs. 39, 58 & 72.*

## Gall Bladder Discomforts

Where there is no tenderness but only pain, any effective site or multiples of them can be used. For the upper abdomen wrist-hand point 5 (fig. 82) is a non-specific point. Knee point 7 (fig. 83) can be used for gall bladder discomforts.

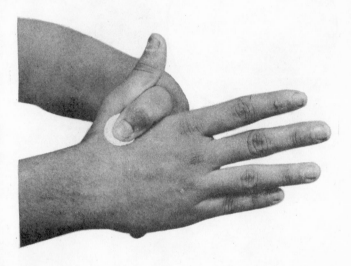

*Fig. 82*
**Wrist-hand Point 5** *(Large Intestine 4) : It is located midway between the two bones of thumbs and index finger. One can find it by closing the thumb and the forefinger together and noticing the little mound that forms at their junction on the back of the hand. The point lies under the peak of the little mound. It can also be found by bending the thumb of the other hand over the web between the thumb and the index finger as shown in the illustration. The point lies under the end of the thumb. End of thumb is directly on site. See also Figs. 20, 63, 69, 76 & 92.*

In cases of acute gall bladder disease, knee point 7 (fig. 83) may be tender itself. In that event pressure with care should be applied.

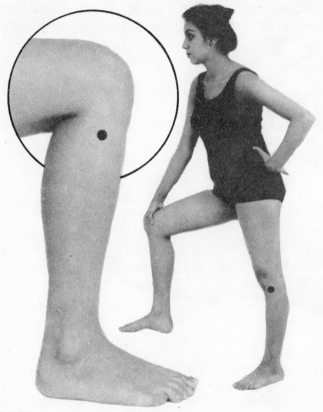

Fig. 83
**Knee Point 7** (Gall Bladder 34) : Located in front of and below the head of the fibula which is the rounded knob located near the middle of the outside aspect of the leg at a level about two finger breadths below the lower level of the knee cap. The point itself is located in the depressed area in front of and below the fibula head. See also fig. 33.

Leg point 1 (fig. 84) and back point 7 (fig. 85) are points that can be used for upper abdominal pains, including those from peptic ulcers, indigestion and chronic gall bladder disease.

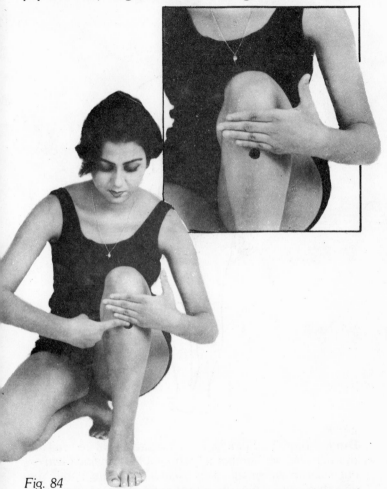

Fig. 84
**Leg Point 1** (Stomach 36): Located for finger-breadhs below the lower level of the knee cap and about one finger breadth to the outside of the shin bone in the soft tissue there. See also fig. 49.

Since they do not overlie the problem directly but are remote, firm pressure and massage can be used.

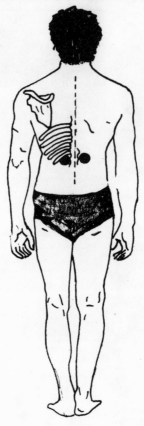

Fig. 85
**Back Point 7** *(Bladder 21)* : *Located between twelfth thoracic and first lumbar vertebrae. One can find them on each side of the spinal column, each point lying about two fingerbreadths to the side of the middle of the spinal column. Points are located three fingerbreadths above the lowest level of the rib cage.*

# 18

# Asthma and Cough including Hiccoughs

These conditions should only be treated under a physician's supervision. However, after a diagnosis and with your physician's consent — or in an emergency while waiting for a physician to arrive — pressure and massage over these acupuncture sites may be beneficial for relief

Chest point 1 (fig. 86) may be pressed and massaged on both sides. Elbow point 2 (fig. 87) and wrist-hand point 1 (fig. 88) also may be pressed and massaged unilaterally or bilaterally.

Other points are also useful for cough or asthma including some points on or near the back to the chest. (See next page).

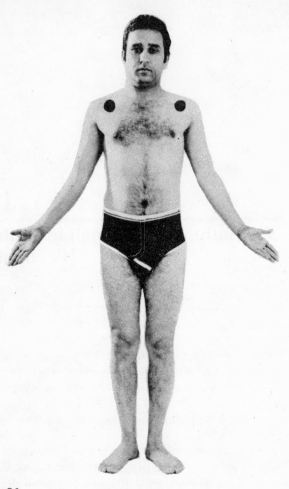

*Fig. 86*
**Chest Point 1** *(Lung 1): Measure two inches from the nipple (in the direction of the arm). Count up three ribs. The point is between the first and second ribs from the top, one inch below the middle of the clavicle the collarbone.*

Fig. 87
**Elbow Point 2** (Lung 5): *Located in the elbow fold in the radial side of the biceps. See also fig. 5.*

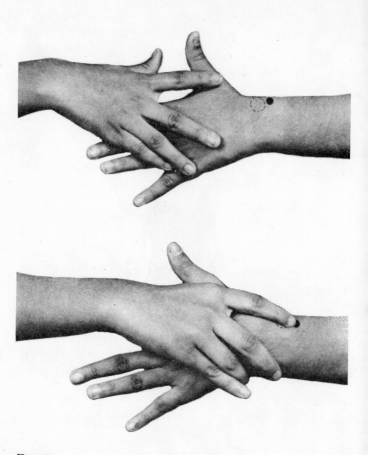

Fig. 88
**Wrist-hand Point 1** (Lung 7) : Located on the thumb side of the wrist just above the radial tuberosity (a projection of bone just above the thumb side of the wrist).Can be found by placing the hands as shown in the illustration. It is about 2 fingerbreadths above the wrist fold. Site is directly under tip of Index finger. See also fig. 16 & 64.

These points include neck point 2 (fig. 89) and back point 6 (fig. 90). Back point 6 is especially useful, pressed bilaterally, for cough. The aid of a friend is needed.

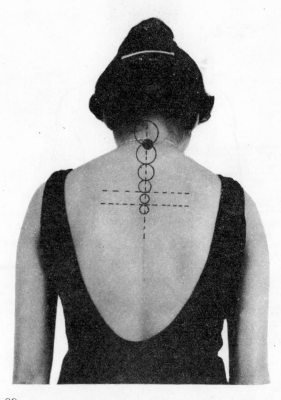

Fig. 89
**Neck Point 2** *(Covering Vessel 14): Locate by bending the neck slightly and noting prominent bone at base of neck. Point is located just below this prominent vertebral spine in the space in between it and the next lower (and less prominent) vertebral or back bone spine. See also fig. 46.*

Another point is neck point 1 (fig. 91) which we encountered previously for sorethroats and "getting something down the Sunday throat."

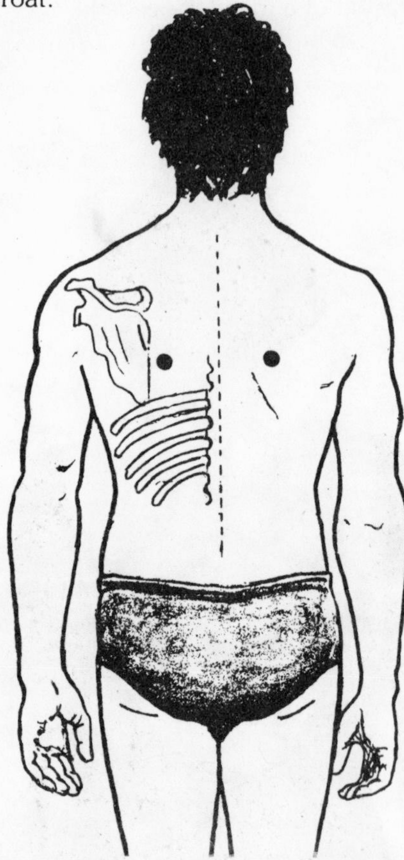

Fig. 90
**Back Point 6** (Bladder 43): Located between fourth and fifth thoracic vertebrae. One can find them on each side of the middle side of the shoulder blade (scapula), not over the bone but in the soft tissue near its edge about half way down the shoulder blade or four fingerbreadths above the lowest level of the shoulder blade.

## Hiccoughs

Another thing for which this point is useful is hiccoughs. Press firmly and you will be surprised how often it will work.

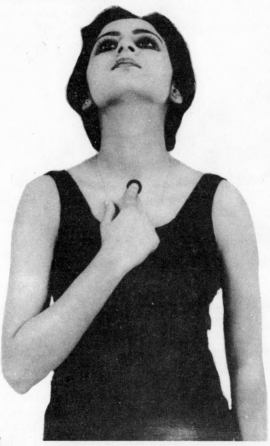

Fig. 91
**Neck Point 1** (Conception Vessel 22) : Located just above the sternal notch or just above the breast bone where the soft tissue of the front of the neck begins. Site is directly under tip of Index finger. See also Fig. 79.

119

Our old friend wrist-hand point 5 (fig. 92) is also useful for asthma. For any individual who hopes to get relief from pressure points, there are numerous points as shown in this section. Trial and error to find the most advantageous ones must be tried. The most effective ones can then be employed when found.

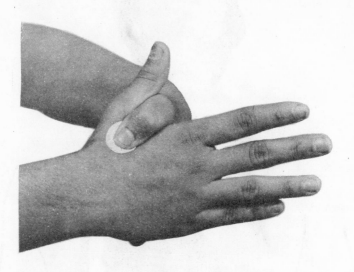

*Fig. 92*

**Wrist-hand Point 5** *(Large Intestine 4) : It is located midway between the two bones of thumbs and index finger. One can find it by closing the thumb and the forefinger together and noticing the little mound that forms at their junction on the back of the hand. The point lies under the peak of the little mound. It can also be found by bending the thumb of the other hand over the web between the thumb and the index finger as shown in the illustration. The point lies under the end of the thumb. Thumb is directly on site. See also fig. 20, 63, 69, 76 & 82.*

Back point 8 (fig. 93) is good for coughing and asthma.

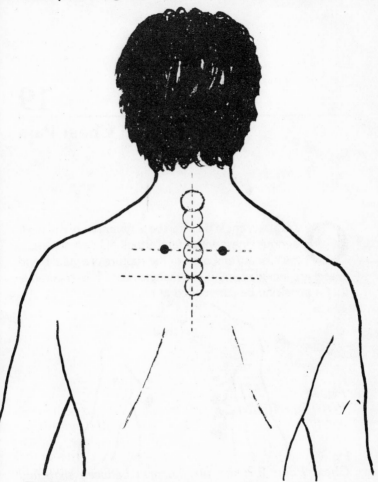

Fig. 93
**Back Point 8**   *(Bladder 13): Located between third and fourth thoracic vertebrae. One can find by finding the large prominent bone on the base of the back of the neck and counting down three additional spines. Point is on each side of the spine two fingerbreadths distance.*

# 19

## Chest Pain

O f course, chest pain can be a symptom of the most serious illness with a fatal attack of heart disease, a pulmonary embolus, or the rupture of a great blood vessel are included among its many causes. It is imperative that a physician be summoned at once.

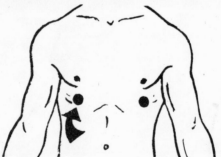

Fig. 94

**Chest Point 2** (Liver 14): *Located between sixth and seventh ribs, directly under the nipple. Other way of finding them is by detecting two ribs below the nipple on about a vertical line travelling through the middle of the natural position of the nipple (in a woman lying on her black with the breast positioned so that it is symetrical with the nipple in the middle)*

Chest point 2 (fig. 94) is good for rib pain or intercostal neuralgia. Use bilaterally with pressure and massage, if desired. Wrist-hand point 3 (fig. 95) is also effective.

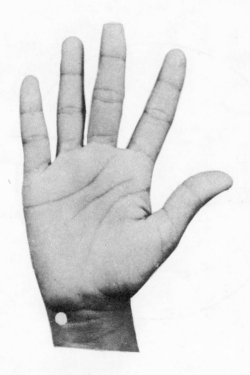

Fig. 95
**Wrist-hand Point 3** (Heart 7) : Located on the palmar aspect of the wrist at the first crease after the hand-wrist junction crease on the little finger side of the hand. (Seven eights of the width of the wrist from the thumb side). See also figs. 18 & 75.

Wrist-hand point 10 (fig. 96) also can be used in chest pain, including angina with your doctor's consent.

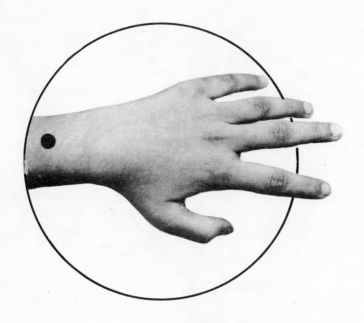

Fig. 96
**Wrist-hand Point 10** (Tripple Burner 5) : Located on the back side or the forearm three fingerbreadths above the middle of the wrist crease. See also fig. 25.

# 20

# Bed Wetting

This point, finger point 1 (fig. 97), is used for bed wetting (nocturia). The child's finger, as indicated below, should be pressed for several minutes at his bedtime. He should empty his bladder at that time. Awaken him about midnight and again have him empty his bladder and again press the finger point several minutes. Repeat the procedure nightly until there has been no successive bedwetting for at least an entire week.

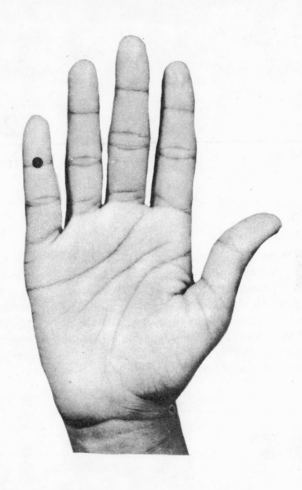

Fig. 97
**Finger Point 1** (Nocturia Point) : Located on the palm side
of the little finger over the middle of the most distant crease
from the palm.

# 21

# Fainting (Syncope)

The following two points may be used to rouse a person in a faint. They are face point 10 (fig. 98) and face point 3 (fig. 99) unilaterally or bilaterally. Face point 10 also can be used alone or in conjunction with face point 9 (fig. 68) to stifle a sneeze.

Fig. 98
**Face-Point 10** (Governing Vessel 26): Located midway between the bottom of the nose and the top of the upper lip.

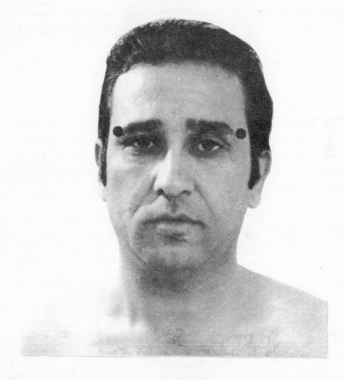

Fig. 99
**Face Point 3** (Tripple Burner 23): Located on each side of
the forehead at the outer edge of the eyebrows. See also
Fig. 62.

Removing the shoes and pressing hard on ankle-foot point 8 (fig. 100) also may be of use for fainting. It may be done bilaterally for best results. A doctor should be consulted about fainting regardless of the speculation as to its cause.

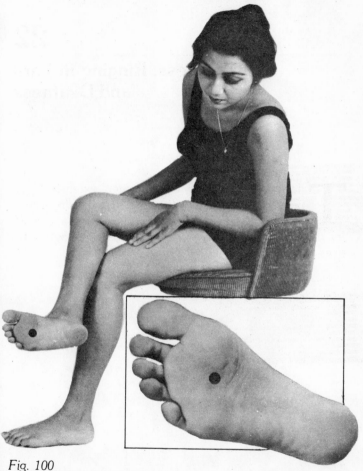

Fig. 100
**Ankle-foot Point 8** (Kidney 1) : Located one third of the way from the toes to the heel on the bottom of the foot in the midline.

# 22

## Dizziness, Ringing in Ears and Deafness

**T**hese maladies have been treated extensively by needle acupuncture with success ranging from zero to the miraculous, Treating nerve deafness, at least for the present should be left to the physician whether he uses acupuncture or not.

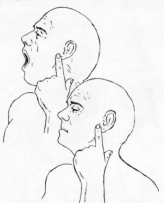

*Fig. 101*
**Face Point 5** *(Gall Bladder 2) : Located on each side of the face by opening the mouth wide and feeling the depression formed in front of the ears at the top of the ear lobe level. Press the point with the mouth closed. See also Fig. 71.*

Three pressure points will be mentioned here for use in treating either dizziness or ringing in the ears. The first point, ankle-foot point 7 (fig. 102), is used best for dizziness.

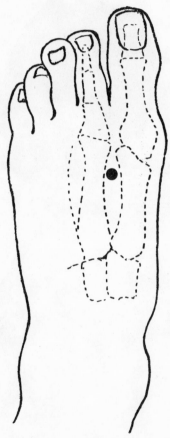

Fig. 102
**Ankle-foot Point** (Liver 3): Located two finger breadths above the base of the toes in between the bony extension of the large toe and second toe.

The other two, face point 5 (fig. 101) and face point 1 (fig. 103), are acupuncture sites used for treating ringing in ears, as well as for other things. They may be tried for dizziness also.

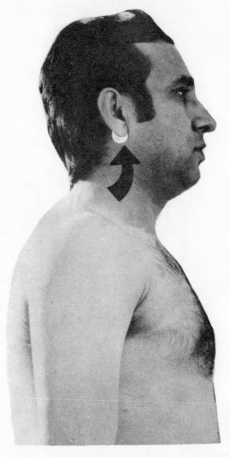

Fig. 103
**Face Point 11** (Tripple Burner 17): Behind the ear lobe just in front of the rounded mastoid bone.

# 23

## Excessive Sweating or Polyhydrosis

**W**rist-hand point 12 (fig. 104) should be pressed hard bilaterally to prevent sweating, especially of the type associated with nervousness and the menopause. Do it for 5 or 10 minutes either before an anticipated sweat or to stop it once it has started. Wrist-hand point 5 (figs. 63, 69, 76, 82, 92) can also be used. The two points may be pressed simultaneously, with the middle finger on wrist-hand point 12, and the thumb on wrist-hand point 5. Be sure to push straight down on each point

Fig. 104
**Wrist-hand Point 12** *(Polyhydrosis Point): Located over the centre of the palm.*

# 24

# Urinary Problems, Constipation, Diarrhea, Strokes, and Hypertension

The points that have been described in this book encompass the most fundamental, commonly used points in acupuncture. As such they have many uses not specifically described thus far in the book. A series of illnesses, some serious, are listed below wherein these points are used. Consultation by a physician must be sought before these points are relied upon.

Urinary problems including prostate, bladder and kidney
1. Abdomen Point 4 (Figs. 59 & 80)
2. Knee Point 7 (Figs. 33, 83)
3. Ankle-foot Point 6 (Figs. 39, 58, 72, 81)
4. Ankle-foot Point 3 (Fig. 36)
5. Back Point 1 (Figs. 8, 55)

Constipation:
1. Leg Point 1 (Figs. 49, 84)
2. Ankle-foot Point 2 (Fig. 35)
3. Abdomen Point 3 (Fig. 73)

Diarrhea:
1. Ankle-foot Point 6 (Figs. 39, 58, 72, 81)
2. Wrist-hand Point 5 (Figs. 20, 63, 69, 76, 82, 92)

3. Abdomen Point 4 (Figs. 59, 80)
4. Umbilicus
5. Knee Point 5 (Figs. 31, 73)

Visual disturbances including Glaucoma:
1. Face Point 3 (Figs. 62, 99)
2. Face Point 2 (Fig. 66)
3. Wrist-hand Point 5 (Figs. 20, 63, 69, 76, 82, 92)
4. Back Point 1 (Figs. 8, 55)

Convalescence from strokes (weakness or paralysis) involving face:
1. Face Point 6 (Fig. 65)
2. Face Point 8 (Fig. 70)
3. Face Point 7 (Fig. 67)
4. The points just to each side of the lip

Involving upper extremity:
1. Elbow Point 4 (Fig. 4)
2. Elbow Point 3 (Fig. 3)
3. Wrist-hand Point 5 (Figs. 20, 63, 69, 75, 82, 92)
4. Wrist-hand Point 1 (Figs. 16, 64, 88)

Lower Extremity:
1. Knee Point 7 (Figs. 33, 83)
2. Ankle-foot Point 1 (Fig. 34)
3. Knee Point 5 (Figs. 31, 73)
4. Leg Point 2 (Fig. 14)
5. Leg Point 1 (Figs. 49, 84)

Hypertension (High Blood Pressure):
1. The key point is at the middle of the hairline in front directly above face point 1 (Fig. 61) (For bald people it is where the hairline was originally)
2. Face Point 1 (Fig. 61)
3. Elbow Point 1 (Fig. 3)
4. Face Point 2 (Fig. 65)
5. Leg Point 1 (Figs. 49, 84)

# PRESSURE POINTS

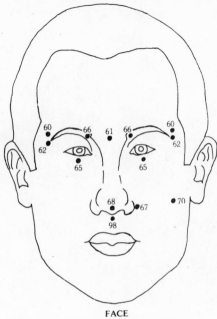

**FACE**

| ILLUS NO. | CHINESE MERIDIAN NAME | ANATOMICAL NAME | TECHNIQUE & TREATMENT |
|---|---|---|---|
| 60 | Sun X | Face Point 4 | For **red swollen eyes** and **dizziness** press these points with one thumb gradually and hard 7-10 seconds, three times. See Page 83 |
| 61 | Governing Vessel 24.5 | Face Point 1 | See Page 84 |
| 62 | Tripple Burner 23 | Face Point 3 | See Pages 85, 128 |
| 65 | Stomach 2 | Face Point 6 | See Page 88 |
| 66 | Bladder 2 | Face Point 2 | See Page 89 |
| 67 | Large Intestine 20 | Face Point 7 | For **nasal obstruction, running nose, facial tension** press hard and inward at a 45° angle with the index finger for 10-15 seconds, three times. See Page 90 |
| 68 | Governing Vessel 25 | Face Point 9 | See Page 91 |
| 70 | Stomach 6 | Face Point 8 | See Page 94 |
| 98 | Governing Vessel 26 | Face Point 10 | For **loss of consciousness, epilepsy** press hard and inward with index finger or a pointed object for 7-10 seconds, three times. See Page 127 |

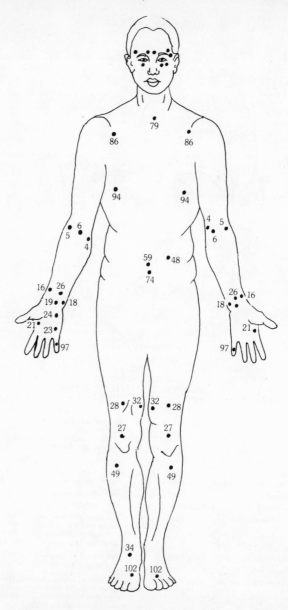

| 4 | Heart 3 | Elbow Point 4 | Stimulation of Elbow Point 4 alone can also be effective for heart palpitation. If this point is pressed with one thumb, hard, 7-10 seconds, three times, it gives relief to **cough, elbow pain** and **laboured breathing.** See Page 21 |
|---|---|---|---|
| 5 | Lung 5 | Elbow Point 2 | See Pages 22, 115 |
| 6 | Paricardium 3 | Elbow Point 3 | See Page 23 |
| 16 | Lung 7 | Wrist-hand Point 1 | Press Wrist-hand Point 1 with one thumb hard and inward 7-10 seconds, three times. This will relieve you of **common colds, headaches** and **Bell's palsy.** See Page 36 |
| 18 | Heart 7 | Wrist-hand Point 3 | If pressed hard and inward with one thumb for 5-7 seconds three times, it helps **reviving an unconscious patient, insomnia, irritability** and **constipation.** See Page 38 |
| 19 | Pericardium 7 | Wrist-hand Point 4 | See Page 39 |
| 21 | Large Intestine 3 | Wrist-hand Point 6 | See Page 41 |
| 23 | Small Intestine 3 | Wrist-hand Point 8 | See Page 43 |
| 24 | Small Intestine 4 | Wrist-hand Point 9 | See Page 43 |
| 26 | Pericardium 6 | Wrist-hand Point 11 | See Pages 45 |
| 27 | Stomach 35 | Knee Point 1 | See Page 47 |
| 28 | Stomach 34 | Knee Point 2 | If pressed hard and inward with one thumb for 7-10 seconds, three times, **stomach pains, diarrhea, arthritis in the knee** get much relief. See Page 48 |
| 32 | Spleen 10 | Knee Point 6 | For **itching, neurodermatitis, hives, menstrual pain** press hard and inward with one thumb for 5-7 seconds, three times. You'll get sure relief. See Page 52 |
| 34 | Stomach 41 | Ankle-foot Point 1 | See Page 55 |
| 48 | Stomach 21 | Abdomen Point 1 | See Page 70 |
| 49 | Stomach 36 | Leg Point 1 | For **general well-being** and **tired legs** press hard and inward with two thumbs for 10-15 seconds, three times. See Page 71 |
| 59 | Conception Vessel 4 | Abdomen Point 4 | For **menstrual cramps, frigidity** press this point inward gradually and deeply with palm of hand for 10-15 seconds, three times. See Page 81 |
| 74 | Conception Vessel 6 | Abdomen Point 3 | For **stomach pains, diarrhea, wet dreams, constipation** etc., press inward, gradually and deeply with palm of your hand for 10-15 seconds, three times. See Page 99 |
| 79 | Conception Vessel 22 | Neck Point 1 | See Pages 106, 119 |
| 86 | Lung 1 | Chest Point 1 | See Page 114 |
| 94 | Liver 14 | Chest Point 2 | For **rib pain, poor lactation** in nursing mothers press these points softly and inward with one thumb for 5-10 seconds, three times. See Page 122 |
| 97 | Nocturia Point | Finger Point 1 | See Page 126 |
| 102 | Liver 3 | Ankle-foot Point 7 | See Page 131 |

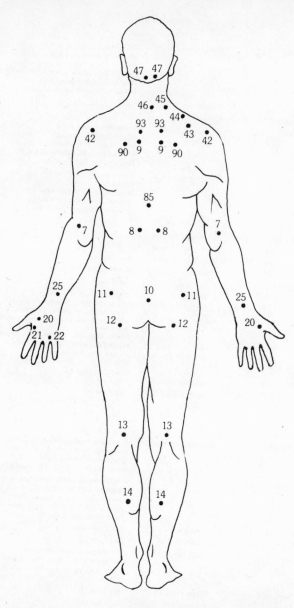

| | | |
|---|---|---|
| 7 | Tripple Burner 10 | Elbow Point 5 |
| 8 | Bladder 23 | Back Point 1 |

See Page 24

If these points are pressed with one thumb, avoiding any sudden pressure. for 7-10 seconds, three times **headache** and **nasal obstruction** also get relief. See Page 26

| | | |
|---|---|---|
| 9 | Trigger Points | Back Point 2 |
| 10 | Governing Vessel 1&2 | Back Point 3 |
| 11 | Gall Bladder 30 | Back Point 4 |
| 12 | Bladder 51 | Back Point 5 |
| 13 | Bladder 54 | Knee Point 4 |
| 14 | Bladder 57 | Leg Point 2 |

See Page 28

See Page 29

See Page 30

See Page 31

See Pages· 32 ,50·

Press softly and inward with one thumb for 10-15 seconds and get relieved of **sciatica, muscle spasms,** and tired legs. See Page 33

| | | |
|---|---|---|
| 20 | Large Intestine 4 | Wrist-hand Point 5 |

If pressed hard with one thumb towards the index finger for 10-15 seconds, three times, one gets relief from **diarrhea, rash, pain of toothache, facial tension** which all are good and important for general health. See Page 40

| | | |
|---|---|---|
| 21 | Large Intestine 3 | Wrist-hand Point 6 |
| 22 | Tripple Burner 2 | Wrist-hand Point 7 |
| 25 | Tripple Burner 5 | Wrist-hand Point 10 |
| 42 | Tripple Burner 14 | Shoulder Point 3 |
| 43 | Small Intestine 12 | Shoulder Point 4 |
| 44 | Gall Bladder 21 | Shoulder Point 5 |

See Page 41

See Page 42

See Page 44

See Page 63

See Page 64

For **lack of milk in nursing mothers** press firmly but gradually inward with one thumb for 10-15 seconds, three times. It will prove very effective. See Page 65

| | | |
|---|---|---|
| 45 | Small Intestine 15 | Shoulder Point 6 |
| 46 | Governing Vessel 14 | Neck Point 2 |

See Page 66

For **fever, headaches, cold, allergies, asthma** press this point inward and hard, three times.

See Page 67

| | | |
|---|---|---|
| 47 | Bladder 10 | Neck Point 3 |

Cures **headaches** and **nasal obstruction** if these points are pressed with one thumb avoiding any sudden pressure for 7-10 seconds. three times. See Page 68

| | | |
|---|---|---|
| 85 | Bladder 21 | Back Point 7 |
| 90 | Bladder 43 | Back Point 6 |

See Page 112

For **poor circulation** press these points hard and inward with two thumbs for 5-7 seconds, three times.

See Page 118

| | | |
|---|---|---|
| 93 | Bladder 13 | Back Point 8 |

For **breathing problems** press these points hard and inward with two thumbs for 5-7 seconds, three times.

See Page 121

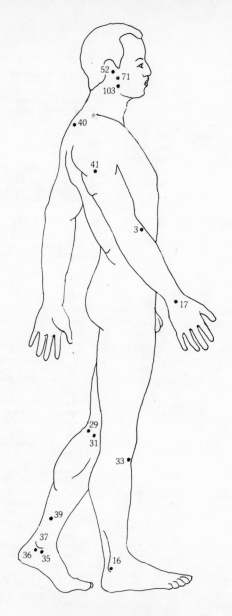

| | | | |
|---|---|---|---|
| 3 | Large Intestine 11 | Elbow Point 1 | It also gives relief to **any arm problem.** See Page 20 |
| 15 | Bladder 60 | Ankle-foot Point 5 | If this point is pressed hard and inward with one thumb for 7-10 seconds, three times, one gets relieved of **sciatica, dizziness** and **epilepsy.** See Page 34 |
| 17 | Tripple Burner 4 | Wrist-hand Point 2 | See Page 37 |
| 29 | Liver 8 | Knee Point 3 | See Pages 49, 78 |
| 31 | Spleen 9 | Knee Point 5 | See Pages 51, 98. |
| 33 | Gall Bladder 34 | Knee Point 7 | **Ankle pain, headache** get relief when this point is pressed hard and inward with one thumb for 7-10 seconds, three times. See Page 53 |
| 35 | Spleen 5 | Ankle-foot Point 2 | See Page 56 |
| 36 | Kidney 6 | Ankle-foot Point 3 | See Page 56 |
| 37 | Kidney 3 | Ankle-foot Point 4 | For **kidney malfunctions** one should press this point hard and inward with one thumb for 7-10 seconds, three times. See Page 57 |
| 39 | Spleen 6 | Ankle-foot Point 6 | Apart from **pain in the ankle, insomnia, overweight, digestive problems, menstrual pain** or **any female sexual problem** also get relief if this point is pressed hard and inward with one thumb for 5-7 seconds, three times. See Page 59 |
| 40 | Large Intestine 15 | Shoulder Point 1 | See Page 61 |
| 41 | Large Intestine 14 | Shoulder Point 2 | See Page 62 |
| 52 | Pericardium 6 | Ear Point 1 | See Page 74 |
| 71 | Gall Bladder 2 | Face Point 5 | For **ringing in the ears** press hard and inward with index finger for 7-10 seconds, three times. See Page 95 |
| 103 | Tripple Burner 17 | Face Point 11 | See Page 132 |

# Health Care in Orient Paperbacks

| | | |
|---|---|---|
| The Complete Book of Home Remedies | Hakeem Abdul Hameed | 50.00 |
| The Complete Book of Family Homoeopathic Medicine | Dr. M.B. Panos & J. Heimlich | 60.00 |
| Home Guide to Medical Emergencies *(Illus)* | Dr. H.J. Heimlich | 50.00 |
| The Complete Book of Yoga *(Illus)* | Sri Ananda | 50.00 |
| Yoga : For Easier Pregnancy & Natural Childbirth *(Illus)* | Sri Ananda | 50.00 |
| Breast Self-Examination *(Illus)* | Dr. Albert R Milan | 45.00 |
| Mental Tension & Its Cure | Dr. O.P. Jaggi | 25.00 |
| Asthma & Allergies : Causes, Prevention & Treatment | Dr. O.P. Jaggi | 30.00 |
| High Blood Pressure : Causes, Prevention & Treatment | Dr. B.K. Mehra | 30.00 |
| Diabetes : Causes, Prevention & Treatment | Ada P Kahn | 30.00 |
| Everyday Eyecare *(Illus)* | Dr. M.S. Aggarwal | 30.00 |
| Better Eyesight Without Glasses | Dr. W.H. Bates | 25.00 |
| The Healthy Heart Cook Book | Dr. H.S. Rajput & Aroona Reejhsinghani | 30.00 |
| Foods That Heal : The Natural Way to Good Health | H.K. Bakhru | 35.00 |
| Yogic Pranayama : Breathing for Long Life and Good Health *(Illus)* | Dr. K.S. Joshi | 40.00 |
| Yogic Cure for Common Diseases *(Illus)* | Dr. Phulgenda Sinha | 35.00 |

*Available at all bookshops or by VPP*

# ORIENT PAPERBACKS

Madarsa Road, Kashmere Gate, Delhi-110006